Vive La Différence

Vive La Différence

A Celebration of the Sexes

Anthony Walsh & Grace J. Walsh

Prometheus Books

59 John Glenn Drive
Buffalo, New York 14228-2197

Published 1993 by Prometheus Books

97 96 95 94 93   5 4 3 2 1

Library of Congress Cataloging-in-Publication Data

Walsh, Anthony, 1941–
    Vive la différence : a celebration of the sexes / Anthony Walsh and Grace J. Walsh.
       p.   cm. — (New concepts in human sexuality series)
    Includes bibliographical references.
    ISBN 0-87975-852-X (cloth)
    1. Sex role. 2. Sex differences 3. Sex. I. Walsh, Grace J. II. Title. III. Series.
HQ1075.W35   1993
305.3—dc20   93-8810
                                                                      CIP

Printed in the United States of America on acid-free paper.

Contents

Vive la différence!!!

Preface

What was the first question anyone ever asked about you? That's right: "Is it a boy or a girl?" And if you were to be suddenly transported across time and space to land in any human culture that ever existed, what would be the first thing the natives would notice about you? In a flash, they would identify you as male or female. No single fact about you is more significant than your sex. Your sex would largely determine how your hosts treated you, just as you were treated differently by your relatives and other interested parties after they found out you were a boy or a girl. Your sex carries with it many ideas and expectations that have remained fairly constant across time and place. Men are men and women are women. Despite large variations in characteristics within each sex, if you are female your hosts would be aware that you are quite a different creature than you would be if you were a male.

Although you inhabit a two-sex world from the moment of conception to the day of your death, psychologically you inhabit a single-sex world. Your sex has charted the course of your physical development, and in many ways the activities you enjoy, the pattern of your relationships, your health, your traits, attitudes, thinking patterns, and behavior. Part of this difference is fashioned from the upbringing you had, and part from your biology. The messages you receive from others in the course of your upbringing are largely determined by your sex, and how receptive you are to these messages is most assuredly determined by it. You cannot fashion a male out of female cloth, or vice versa, no matter how hard you try.

The past few decades have been gender-benders in which some folks have tried to drown sex differences in a sea of androgyny. Many vocal

7

feminists, and some social scientists (who should know better), would like us to believe that apart from the obvious plumbing differences, men and women are pretty much the same. Sure, some women now cuss like troopers and aim Mack trucks down the highway, and some men have been persuaded to eat quiche and to trash their white Jockeys in favor of flowery chartreuse hammocks, but these are superficial reversals of cultural stereotypes.

The study of sex differences is controversial, especially when biology is held to be primarily responsible for them. We are well aware that culture has a lot to do with sex differences, but culture is not the whole story, and neither is biology. In emphasizing biology and difference we want to balance the views of the gender-benders who emphasize culture and similarity.

While culturists were doing their damnedest to blunt the sexual line, the "cutting edge" sciences of human behavior—behavioral genetics, psychobiology, neurophysiology—were quietly sharpening it. Underneath all the unisex hype of the past twenty or so years, it turns out that men and women are still profoundly different creatures. In fact, there are more differences between human males and females than between males and females of any other species. That's because we are such complicated creatures—we have so much more to be different about. If we look just at those sex differences that we share with other species, such as body size, sexual behavior, and so forth, we are less different than males and females of any other species. But it is the differences between the sexes that excite and interest us, not the similarities. There are many mean-spirited books touting a dull, sex-neutral ideal that denies and decries our differences. We want to balance such material by celebrating them: *Vive la différence!*

Let's not make the mistake of thinking superior or inferior when we see the word *different*. The terms *superior* and *inferior* mean that some value judgment has been made about some existing difference, but *difference* simply means "not the same as." If you must think in terms of superiority or inferiority, do it for yourself. Our aim is to present interesting sexual differences in a light-hearted way without passing judgment on them (well, not *too* much). We hope you will accept in the same manner. What needs to be changed is not that which cannot be changed, but rather the value we place on our sex differences.

We have to get one thing straight right away: there is tremendous overlap between the sexes on most of the traits we'll be talking about. If we say something like "women do such and such," it only means that women *in general* tend to do it more often than men. It certainly doesn't mean that all women do it, or that no men do. Take a readily observable trait such as height. To say that "men are taller than women" is to state a generality that by no means denies that some women are taller than some men. It simply means that the "average" man (5'9") is taller than the "average" woman (5'4").

This book was written first and foremost to be informative and entertaining. The material in it is the result of years of collecting information from books, magazines, surveys, newspapers, scientific journals, and various other sources. As active researchers in this area, some of the information comes from our own work. We have endeavored to present scientific generalities from studies that have been repeated, but we have not hesitated to include interesting tid-bits of information that have not. One-time surveys and laboratory studies are not as reliable as work that has been widely replicated, and the validity of surveys is very sensitive to the size of the sample. Although there is strength in numbers, more important than sample size is representativeness. A small sample of about a hundred people that is truly representative of the population from which it was taken is better than an unrepresentative sample many times larger. Samples that do not meet scientific selection criteria may literally be "polls" apart in their findings.

Another thing you must be wary of is sex-based selective answering. It appears that both men and women will answer poll questions differently according to the sex of the pollster. Eagleton Institute pollsters found that 84 percent of female respondents gave a pro-choice answer on the abortion issue when asked by a female pollster, but only 64 percent gave a pro-choice answer to a male pollster. Men were also more pro-choice (77 percent) when asked by a woman than when asked by a man (70 percent). Although both sexes adjusted their answers according to the pollster's sex, females were almost three times more likely than males to do so. Thus female responses may be more suspect than male responses on some issues. Please keep these warnings in mind as you read.

Throughout human history it has been the male that has defined and fixed the standards for evaluating the good, the desirable, and the superior among ideas, things, and people. Not surprisingly, men have defined their own sex as the superior one, and they have confused their prejudices with the laws of nature. The female has been seen as simply an appendage to the male. Even the word *woman* denotes a kind of add-on creature. The word is derived from the old English "wif-man" (wif of man), which became "wim-man," and finally "woman." As Genesis 2 put it: "She shall be called Woman, because she was taken out of Man" ("womb-man," perhaps?).

Writing about sex differences by the light shining from the inner reaches of either the male or female psychologies inevitably breeds a kind of short-sightedness however objective one strives to be. Having two authors of opposite sexes working with the same material minimizes this myopic tendency. Both of us enjoy being our respective sexes and the differences they entail, but we've spent many hours arguing about what these differences mean. The material in this book represents a synthesis of the male and female psychologies, at least as they are represented by the two of us. If we. appear to favor the female more than the male, try to see it as perhaps an effort on our part to rectify some of the myths of male superiority that abound in our culture, and in most others. There's only one place in which one sex should be on top of the other (rotating positions, of course), and that's in bed.

1

Genes and Hormones:
The Basics of Sex Differences

This chapter is written for those of you who are not satisfied with just knowing *how* the sexes are different, but would also like to know *why*. These whys lie mainly in our genes, our hormones, and our brains, so it is necessary to know a little about these things. Don't be put off; we'll keep our discussion of these complicated things as simple as possible. But if you tend to get bored with technical details, or if you already know the basic biology of sex differences, give this chapter a miss and enjoy the rest of the book.

GENES: THE SEEDS OF SEX

According to Genesis, man is God's special creation and woman was fashioned as his plaything from one of Adam's less valuable spare parts because "it is not good that man should be alone." It certainly wouldn't be very good if man (or woman, for that matter) were alone, and we are all grateful for God's consideration. But Genesis got it backwards: man, not woman, is nature's afterthought. Femaleness, not maleness, is the "standard" form of humanity. It'll take us a page or two to explain what we mean by this.

A female is born with a relatively small number of eggs (they will develop from a much larger number of potential eggs called follicles), and these are all she will ever have. She will periodically shed them at a typical rate of one a month between puberty, when her potential for child bearing begins, and menopause, when it ends. Her eggs contain twenty-three chromosomes—tiny, threadlike creatures containing the genetic instructions for our physical, and, to a lesser extent, our psychological development. Twenty-two of these chromosomes are called autosomes and they will combine with a similar number of autosomes contributed by the father's sperm to produce the forty-four autosomes that are in every cell in our bodies. The twenty-third chromosome, the sex chromosome, is the one responsible for our sexual characteristics. There are two kinds of sex chromosomes, X and Y. The female egg contains only the X chromosome, the female chromosome.

Unlike the female, the male is constantly producing sperm, billions every day during his prime. Like female eggs, sperm (which are really genes with a delivery system) contain twenty-three chromosomes, but the male produces an equal number of both female X and male Y sex chromosomes. When a healthy male ejaculates he shoots out anywhere from 250 million to 500 million sperm, starting a frantic, thirty-minute race up the vaginal barrel and beyond to be the first to fertilize the waiting egg. To give you some idea of how rough the race is, at least 100 million sperm are needed if conception is to have a fighting chance of occurring because hundreds of thousands perish each step of the way.

You might think that thirty minutes is an awfully long time to make a journey of only about five inches, but to put things in perspective we have to realize the size dimensions involved. The unfertilized egg is about the size of the period at the end of this sentence, but about 85,000 sperm could fit in that same space. So you see why it's quite a struggle for such a little guy or gal. Your life began at that miraculous flash in time when one of them, and only one of them, made it, for this is the ultimate "winner take all" competition. The single sperm, among the twenty or so that made it to the vicinity of the egg, penetrated its membrane and lived on as you; the others simply died. At this point the separate sperm and egg become a *zygote,* a cell formed by their union on its way to making a new and unique person. Your sex was determined by whether it was an X or a Y sperm that won the race.

WHY X DOESN'T EQUAL Y

The majestic X chromosome is a giant compared to the short and stumpy Y, and carries immensely more genetic information—about 5 to 6 percent

The Sperm Sweepstakes

of the total genetic material, the rest of it being carried on the autosomes. Mr. Y, on the other hand, is a virtually empty little creature. The genetic information carried by Ms. X controls the formation of many bodily structures, but apart from some sex-differentiation instructions such as how to start to make a penis and testes, the only structural features so far identified as carried by the Y chromosome are useless and icky. Three structures—webbed toes, hard lesions of the hands and feet, and bark-like skin—are rare. The fourth—hairy ears—bothers most men as they get older. Other defects that afflict only or mostly men are the result of the genetic information the Y does *not* carry rather than what it does.

Having to lug such a heavy load, sperm carrying the X chromosome are slightly less likely to reach to egg first. If an X sperm fertilizes the egg, the result is an XX female, if a Y sperm does, the result is an XY male. We call these genetic patterns male or female *genotypes*. The normal female, then, has two units of femaleness, and the normal male has one unit of femaleness and one unit of maleness. Perhaps George Orwell was right when he wrote that, "All men are born females but some are more female than others." Because the female has only one kind of chromosome to contribute, but the male has two possibilities, a child's sex is determined entirely by its father. A handy way of remembering which chromosomal pattern is associated with which sex is that while the male is seXY, the female *is* seXX.

Given the weight advantage enjoyed by the Y chromosome, about 125 males are conceived for every 100 females. But because the Y chromosome is so small and vulnerable, this disproportion is reduced to about 105 male to 100 female live births as the male excess is weeded out by miscarriages and still births. This figure applies generally to more developed countries; in undeveloped countries with poor nutritional standards there are actually more females born because they are better able to withstand the disabilities associated with poverty. The excess of male conceptions may be even greater than 125 to 100 because these figures are based on miscarriages or still births in which the sex of the fetus could be determined. Some authorities estimate that as many as 150 males are conceived for every female. This pattern of male excess is also seen in many other mammalian species, such as cattle and rats. Males continue to be more vulnerable to illness and death over the lifespan until the male/female ratio more than reverses itself in later life.

GENDER BENDING

When we say that the male is nature's afterthought, we mean that the "basic" human being is female. It is not the presence of the X chromosome that makes a female, it is rather the absence of the Y chromosome. Now and again nature makes a mistake and there are children born with chromosomal patterns other than XX or XY, such as XXX, XXY, or XXXXY. But no matter how many X "units" of femaleness the fetus has, the presence of a single Y results in the male pattern of sexual differentiation. In its ability to assert itself even in the presence of more than one X chromosome, old Y doesn't seem to be such a wimpy fellow after all. On the other hand, the Y chromosome cannot survive without a complementary X chromosome, but the X chromosome can stand alone without either another X or a Y as a mate. Perhaps the feminists' terse sentiment that, "A man without a woman is like a fish without a tail, but a woman without a man is like a fish without a bicycle," finds some support at the chromosomal level.

Turner's syndrome females offer an example of single-chromosome survival. The most common cause of Turner's syndrome is an X-bearing sperm fertilizing a chromosome-empty egg, resulting in an individual with an X0 chromosome pattern (the zero denotes the absence of a second chromosome). Turner's syndrome occurs in about 1 in every 3,000 female births. A Turner's syndrome person is unmistakably female. She is even more feminine in many behavioral and intellectual respects than her XX sisters, although she is infertile. So in a sense the X chromosome is "superior" in both the amount of genetic information it carries and its ability to produce a viable human being in the absence of a mate. On the other hand, the Y chromosome is "superior" in its ability to bully its way to maledom in the presence of any number Xs.

HORMONES AND SEX: WE ARE WHAT WE SECRETE

Biologists have determined that the genetic differences that separate men and women amounts only to about 3 percent, which means that we have 97 percent of our genetic endowment in common. Three percent doesn't sound like much until we realize that only about 2 percent of our genes separate humans from chimpanzees! We don't have to tell you that there's a million different things that differentiate humans from chimps, so a simple comparison of percentages is misleading. The genetic 3 percent that differentiates human males and females is probably mostly tied up in regulating hormone secretions.

Although the presence of the Y chromosome is necessary to produce a male, it is far from sufficient. Certain hormones have to be activated and hormone receptors have to be present to receive them to complete the job. The fact that life is possible without a Y chromosome but impossible without an X, and that a number of additional hormonal processes have to be activated to produce a male, increases our confidence in the conclusion made long ago by Charles Darwin that the basic human being is female.

Some geneticists even find it amusing to think of the Y chromosome as an undeveloped X, or that some time in our long evolutionary history Mr. Y was not the separate and distinct creature he is today, but rather a broken X. (Actually, the Y chromosome looks more like half an "x" than a "Y"). If it is true that Y is really a fractured X, the original break may have been the origin of the necessity for sexual reproduction. There was certainly a time many millions of years ago when the creatures who would end up as human males and females reproduced themselves asexually by self-fertilization. This method is more efficient than (if not nearly as much fun as) sexual reproduction, and is the way most living things reproduce themselves. Such a chromosomal combination—one good X and one fractured Y carrying some unfortunate genes—produced incomplete females, those creatures we now call males.

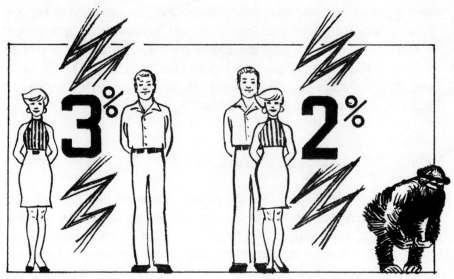

The Gender Gap   The Species Gap

Contrary to what we might think, Y doesn't even carry all the necessary genes to sexually differentiate a male from a female. Normal differentiation into a male requires genetic information carried by its big sister, Ms. X, as well. Recent genetic research suggests that a *single* gene on the Y chromosome is its contribution to maleness. Like Paul Revere, this molecular horseman is responsible for rousing his compatriots to begin the series of tasks that must be carried out to divert the organism away from femaleness and toward maleness. This gene carries the so-called "testis determining factor," the gene responsible for producing the male testes. Every woman has all the genes for making a man except for this one, and every man has all the genes for becoming a women but is diverted from that course by this single gene.

Incidentally, because there are more information-carrying genes on the X chromosome, and because a girl gets an X from her father as well as her mother, she gets more genes from her father than does her brother. Her brother, on the other hand, gets more genetic material from his mother (the single X chromosome). This is the reason that boys are somewhat more likely than girls to facially resemble their mothers. Children's resemblances to their father that are not related to sexual differentiation come from the autosomes he gave them. Another indication of this is the degree of association between mother/daughter, father/daughter, mother/son, and father/son IQs. Parent and offspring in each of the first three instances have an X chromosome in common, but father and son have no such common X, the son's sole X coming from his mother. As expected, the degree of parent/child IQ association is quite large in the first three cases, but is only moderate between father and son.

We may break the process of sexual differentiation down into two stages. The first stage—genetic sex—is determined by whether the egg was fertilized by an X or by a Y chromosome. The second stage—gonadal sex—involves the development of the gonads into the male testes or female ovaries. You might think that genetic males and females carry separate and distinct genetic instructions governing the development of male and female genitalia. This is not the case at all. Both sets of genetic "blueprints" carry identical information, but are acted on or suppressed according to

the interaction of a number of genes. Both XX and XY fetuses have rudimentary gonads and a genital tubercle from which the testes, ovaries, penis, and clitoris will emerge. At this stage of the game these structures are identical. About six weeks after conception, the genetic male will begin to develop testes. After several more weeks a genetic female's ovaries will start to develop.

After the testes are formed they begin to secrete hormones—a word derived from the Greek for "to arouse"—that will organize the development of the internal and external male genitalia. These organizing hormones are the incredibly powerful male androgens, the most important of which is testosterone. This word can be roughly said to mean a testes-producing sterol (all sex hormones are manufactured from cholesterol. the stuff that clogs our arteries). The female ovaries also begin to secrete hormones at this time, but these hormones are not responsible for the development of her genitalia as male hormones are responsible for his. Remember, the male is the add-on creature, so there is no hormonal influence necessary to develop the basic human. It is the *absence* of male hormones that allows for the development of the female, not the presence of female hormones, although progesterone may function to protect the female from the diverting influence of the small amount of androgens she secretes.

Unlike the external genitals, the internal reproductive structures do not develop from the same tissue. In this sense all embryos are hermaphrodites, possessing both male Wolffian and female Müllerian ducts. At about three months, androgens from the male testes cause the Wolffian structures to develop into the male internal sex organs—vas deferens, seminal vesicles, and ejaculatory duct. The fetal testes also secrete a chemical called Müllerian inhibiting substance (MIS), which causes the female Müllerian structures to atrophy. Without androgens, the Wolffian structure degenerates, and without MIS the Müllerian structures will develop into the female internal sex organs—uterus, fallopian tubes, and upper portions of the vagina.

NATURE'S MISTAKES

Sometimes the cells of an XY fetus are insensitive to secreted androgens, a condition known as the *androgen insensitivity syndrome* (AIS). When this condition exists the male pattern of development will not occur and the fetus (Y chromosome and all) will develop as a female. In an XY male with AIS, androgen can't do its job developing the Wolffian structures because of cell insensitivity, so there are no internal male organs. But because the testes have developed and begun secreting MIS, MIS has done its job and caused the Müllerian structures to atrophy, so there are no internal female organs either. (The testes of an AIS person do not descend; they remain lodged internally.) To the average person these genetic males appear in almost all respects to be well-formed XX females. They are apparently so good-looking and feminine in their mannerisms that they are overrepresented in comparison to their numbers in the ranks of success-ful models. They are about three inches taller than the average woman, have short vaginas and have no armpit or pubic hair. Lacking internal female organs, AIS individuals don't menstruate and are infertile. Because of their androgen insensitivity, AIS individuals are more feminine in their behavior patterns than normal XX females, who are responsive to the small amounts of androgen they secrete.

An interesting variant of the AIS that drives home the importance of hormones on the way we behave is the *5-alpha-reductase deficiency syndrome* (5aR). Children born with 5aR usually appear at birth to be unambiguous females and are raised as such. Actually, they are XY males who lack the gene that codes for the 5aR enzyme (enzymes are substances that bring about or accelerate reactions and changes in our body cells), which is important to male sex-hormone synthesis. Although these chil-dren have normal male levels of testosterone and MIS, they lack a substance derived from testosterone called dihydrotestosterone because of the miss-ing enzyme. They have all the normal internal male sex organs, including testes, although they are concealed in the groin. At puberty 5aR children undergo a physical transformation to maleness, including growth of the penis and descent of the testes.

Depending on the cultural context (how sex-segregated it is) the ease of transition from the female to the male role ranges from relatively easy to quite traumatic. 5aR individuals in more "enlightened" cultures evi-dently feel a sense of relief in that their bodies now conform to the sex their "inner voices" told them that they were, despite twelve to fourteen years of female rearing. This suggests that although dihydrotestosterone is necessary for the promotion of the external male sex characteristics at birth, testosterone makes for a relatively normal masculine puberty and has a masculinizing effect on the brain to form the normal male gender identity despite the early absence of dihydrotestosterone. 5aR males provide striking evidence that the myth of sexual neutrality at birth is just that.

The importance of the androgens to masculinity is further dramatized in yet another of nature's mistakes, *congenital adrenal hyperplasia* (CAH). CAH is the result of the action of a nondominant (recessive) gene on a nonsex chromosome (autosome); geneticists call such traits autosomal recessive. This genetic action decreases the production of cortisol by the adrenal cortex, which causes increased secretion of androgens from the adrenal glands and results in precocious sexual development in males and the masculinization of the genitalia in females. CAH female infants show varying degrees of clitoral enlargement (sometimes to the point of matching the male penis in size), and varying degrees of closure of the vaginal lips. If these girls are given cortisol treatments and have their reproductive organs surgically corrected, they are fully capable of bearing children. Untreated, they will show further masculinization of the external sex organs. CAH females show significantly more male-typical behavior than normal females, suggesting that their brains had been masculinized to some extent by the excess andrenal testosterone.

Klinefelter's syndrome males are an example of individuals with two or more X chromosomes who nevertheless show the male pattern of development because of the presence of a Y chromosome. Klinefelter males most usually have an XXY chromosome pattern, although other patterns such as XXXY are sometimes found. Klinefelter's boys tend to be born to older mothers, and the syndrome appears to be the result of a fault in the genetic control in cell division in the egg after fertilization. They are undetectable at birth except by a type of genetic test known as karyotyping. They may have smaller than normal testes but a penis that is capable of erection and satisfactory intercourse. As a rule, the ejaculate of these men contains no sperm. They tend to be taller than normal males (an average of 5'10") and to develop relatively well-formed breasts at puberty. They have about half the male post-pubertal amount of testosterone, which accounts for their low level of sexual activity and female pattern of hair growth and loss. Klinefelter's males often have sexual identity problems, and are significantly more likely than XY males to be homosexual, bisexual, transvestites, transexuals, and inmates in prisons and mental hospitals. The risk of mental retardation is greater than among XY males, and becomes more likely the greater the frequency of additional chromosomes.

One additional genetic abnormalitymust be identified—the XYY male. This genetic combination was originally called "Jacob's Criminal Syndrome," but this name has been dropped as an exaggeration. People with this condition have unofficially been tagged "supermales." This is by no means a complimentary term; "exaggerated" rather than "super" would be a more apt prefix. They are taller than normal males (an average of just over 5'11"), have a lower average IQ, poor impulse control, and are less sensitive and involved with others than normal males. About 1.24 XYY males are born per 1,000 male births. A large Danish sample found XYY males to be imprisoned or in psychiatric hospitals at rates exceeding their numbers in the general population by 7.0 and 2.6 times, respectively. Average differences between XYY and XY males on male-typical traits are not as striking as are differences between X0 and XX females on female-typical traits. Although testosterone levels of XYY men are within the normal male range, they have reduced fertility.

You may have decided by now that the simple anatomical definition of sex can be something of a problem. Science has come up with a relatively simple method of determining sex called nuclear sexing. This method takes advantage of the fact that females have two X chromosomes, meaning that. they have body cells containing both maternal and paternal chromosomes with different genetic information. Geneticists call this *genetic mosaicism;* the female is a genetic mosaic, the male is not. It is obvious that the genetic instructions on both Xs cannot be activated and given expression in the same individual, so the genes on one of the Xs are inactivated. Which chromosome is inactivated is randomly determined, with different Xs active in different cells. This random determination is the reason that female identical twins tend to physically differ from each other more than identical male twins, who have only one X each that must be activated.

When a chromosome is inactivated it remains so throughout life. The inactivation of the genes on a chromosome causes a darkly staining material called chromatin to be visible on the cells of females called the Barr body. If stain-testing reveals the Barr body (chromatin), the person is a female, if not, a male. The odd thing about this is that the Turner's syndrome individual is considered a female anatomically and behaviorally, yet she is Barr body negative because of the absence of the second X. The Klinefelter male is Barr body positive because he has two or more Xs. And you thought that determining sex was just a matter of viewing the plumbing!

TRUE HERMAPHRODITES

The people with intersex anomalies we've examined so far are called *pseudohermaphrodites* and their conditions have well-known genetic or hormonal causes. Pseudohermaphrodites have the gonads of one sex or the other; that is, they have either two testes or two ovaries. True hermaphrodites are individuals with both testicular and ovarian tissue, either in the form of one testicle and one ovary or gonads consisting of both testicular and ovarian tissue (ovotestis). The precise cause of true hermaphroditism is not well known, although it is known that it is genetic rather than hormonal in nature. One kind of true hermaphroditism for which the cause is known is XX/XY chimerism. A chimera is an individual organ or part consisting of unrelated genetic material; for example, a plant graft, a composite of genetically unrelated parts, is a chimera.

True hermaphroditism is sometimes the result of human chimerism. What this means is that a single individual has been formed from the fusion of what normally would have developed from two separate zygotes—opposite-sex fraternal twins. This is verified from examining the genetic pattern of such individuals, which is designated most usually as XX/XY. Other chimeric patterns such as XX/XXY, XX/XXYY, and XX/XYY, are known, and there has been one documented case of quadruple mosaicism—X0/XX/XY/XXY. The genetic patterns for Turner's syndrome (X0), a normal female (XX), a normal male (XY), and for Klinefelter's syndrome (XXY) are found in this one person.

The majority (about 70 percent) of true hermaphrodites are not chimeras and have gene patterns indistinguishable from those of normal males and females, i.e., XX or XY. XY hermaphrodites are Barr body negative and XX hermaphrodites are Barr body positive (XX/XY hermaphrodites are Barr body positive, but they have a lower than normal chromatin count). Since both karyotypes have ovarian and testicular tissue, they offer rare proof that ovarian tissue can develop without a second X chromosome and that testicular tissue can develop without a Y chromosome.

How can this happen? To make a long and complicated story short and relatively simple, a gene on the X chromosome similar in structure to the gene on the Y responsible for testis differentiation has been discovered. Since Y-specific DNA (the stuff from which genes are made) is found in XX hermaphrodites, it means that the biological sequences leading to the formation of testicular tissue has been transferred to the X chromosome. Geneticists call this process translocation.

This explains why XX individuals have testicular tissue, but what about XY individuals with ovarian tissue? Just as XX individuals with testicular tissue have gained a sequence they shouldn't have had due to translocation, XY individuals with ovarian tissue have lost a sequence that they should have had due to what geneticists call deletion. They have lost a critical segment on the short arm of the Y that carries the testis-determining factor. Evidently, they have just enough of the sequence to form some testicular tissue, but not enough to prevent the formation of ovarian tissue as well.

Most true hermaphrodites (about 57 percent) are XX rather than XY or chimeras, and approximately 80 percent of XX hermaphrodites have internal female organs capable of sexual functioning and with some potential for fertility. However, stories of self-fertilization—true hermaphrodites who have been both mother and father to a child—or of true hermaphrodites who have been mother to one child and father to another are pure myth. As of 1988 there were only 528 cases of true hermaphroditism documented in the world literature, and pregnancy has been documented in only seven XX true hermaphrodites and in one XX/XY chimera as of 1990. There are no reported cases of male hermaphrodite fertility.

WHAT IT ALL MEANS

This short biology lesson has been a prelude to our discussion of sex differences in behavior and psychological traits. Anatomy may not be destiny, as Freud declared, but it goes a long way toward explaining sex differences in behavioral traits. It may seem strange to use genetic oddities to determine what normal traits and behaviors are for the typical man and woman. However, geneticists often use mutations—extreme deviations from the species norm—to determine what the species norm is, and brain-damaged individuals have proven invaluable to brain scientists in understanding the workings of normal brains. Many scientists likewise believe that genetic and hormonal deviations from the normal man and woman can tell us a lot about what "normal" is.

In true hermaphroditism the genital anatomy runs all the way from approximately normal female (normal to large clitoris and none to slight closure of the vagina) to almost normal male (small to normal penis and full scrotum). The importance of this to understanding sex-typical traits and behavior is that *the degree of masculinization of the genitalia provides an indication of the extent of brain masculinization: the more masculinized the genital features the more likely the brain has been organized along male lines, the more feminine the genital features the less brain masculinization has taken place.* It is mainly this relative degree of brain alteration from feminine to masculine that is responsible for the variations in male and female behavior. This observation pulls us away from thinking in terms of just two "either/or" sexes toward thinking in terms of people who are male and female to greater or lesser extents according to the ebb and flow of circulating prenatal hormones. The great majority of us are pushed squarely into one camp or another, but some of us are mis-categorized. Thus there are "masculine" women and "feminine" men.

Figure 1 presents a continuum running from the extreme of female-typical behavior to the extreme of male-typical behavior. In drawing this continuum we had in mind primarily the traits that probably most distinguish between the sexes—aggression, dominance, and sexuality (from least female to most male) or nurturance, empathy, and altruism (from most female to least male). The pattern is not always as neat and tidy as we've made out here for every sex-based trait. For instance, KS (Klinefelter's syndrome) males are taller and SM ("supermale") males are less fertile than normal males. Neither can we discount the effects of social learning on various traits (or, indeed, the fact that what is learned depends to a great extent on the inherent propensities these people bring with them to the learning environment). But the diagram does serve as a useful guide to the genetic and hormonal basis of the sex differences we will be exploring.

Figure 1. Maleness/Femaleness Genetic/Hormonal Continuum*

TS	AIS	NF	KS	True Hermaphrodites	CAH	5aR	NM	SM
(X0)	(XY)	(XX)	(XXY)	(XX, XY, XX/XY, etc.)	(XX)	(XY)	(XY)	(XYY)

←——————————————————————————————————————→

Femaleness   Maleness

* TS = Turner's syndrome. AIS = androgen insensitivity syndrome. NF = normal female. KS = Klinefelter's syndrome. CAH = congenital adrenal hyperplasia. 5aR = 5-alpha-reductase deficiency syndrome. NM = normal male. SM = "supermale."

2

The Body

"TWIXT TWELVE AND TWENTY": PUBERTY

Puberty is that special time in life when we stop being boys and girls and start to become men and women capable of reproducing ourselves. Psychologically, we call this period *adolescence,* a period which for some of us may persist long after puberty is over. Although puberty is often seen as an abrupt transition from sex-neutrality to manhood or womanhood, the hormonal kettle began simmering at the earliest stages of life. The budding processes we observe during this time happen only after the kettle has boiled.

Girls begin puberty about two years earlier than boys. Its onset can be reliably dated to menarche, a girl's first menstrual period, which usually occurs between the ages of ten and fourteen. No such single event allows us to precisely date its onset for the male. The first sperm-carrying emission (spermarche), which usually occurs between the ages of eleven and thirteen, could serve such a dating function. But unlike menstruation, ejaculation usually requires a helping hand, and we can't tell if sperm are present in semen without special testing. There is a tremendous increase in masturbation accompanying the testosterone surges of puberty, so the onset of this activity could serve as a handy marker. The stickler is that it's a rare young chap who runs to his mother to tell her that he's just ejaculated.

Apart from menstruation, other visible signs of puberty for the female are proudly budding breasts, the pleasant rounding of the buttocks, and the arrival of wisps of pubic hair, which most females like, and underarm and leg hair, which they don't. In the male we see the beginning of facial, chest, and pubic hair, the protrusion of the Adam's apple, often a few boils and acne spots, and wet dreams. Some boys even experience temporary enlargement of the breasts, although, unlike the female, they are not connected to a dairy. The most welcome change is the exquisite joy of penis elongation, which, full of the novelty of it all, often chooses the most inopportune times to erect itself.

Earlier we saw that the *organizational* stage of sexual differentiation occurred during gestation. Puberty is the second time in our lives in which hormones have a rather sudden, decisive, and unquestionable impact. The hormonal burst is the *activation* stage, the point at which we begin to put the organizational properties into action. Prior to puberty, both sexes have about the same level of testosterone. As girls mature into women, their testosterone level just about doubles, but as boys mature into men, their testosterone levels increase ten to twenty times.

Testosterone levels can't be addressed without knowing something about a substance called sex hormone binding globulin (SHBG). The activating power of hormones depends on their free availability. Most of the body's sex hormones are reversibly bound to this substance, and so not immediately available for use. Before puberty, both sexes have about the same level of SHBG. After puberty, males have about half as much as females, meaning that there are higher concentrations of "free" gonadal hormones available to them. So although adult males have about fifteen to twenty times more testosterone than adult women, they actually have thirty to forty times more "free" testosterone floating around in their blood available for behavioral activation.

CHOLESTEROL: THE GOOD, THE BAD, AND THE UGLY

We've all heard about good and bad cholesterol. High density lipoprotein cholesterol (HDL) is "good" cholesterol, so called because it picks up excess cholesterol and transports it for removal from the body. Low density lipoprotein cholesterol (LDL) is "bad" cholesterol because it collects excess cholesterol and deposits it in our cells, including the blood vessels. Prior to puberty both sexes have about the same levels of cholesterol, but when boys hit puberty and testosterone levels kick in with a vengeance, their HDL levels plunge and their LDL levels start a slow but steady rise. LDL levels also start to rise in girls, but at a slower rate, and their HDL levels hold steady. On average, HDL levels are 25 percent higher in women than in men. This is one of the reasons that women are at a lower risk of heart attack during their younger years.

Female reproduction requirements are behind women's more favorable cholesterol ratio. A pregnant women and her fetus require extra blood and extra carbohydrates, and for this she needs more pliable arteries to manage the extra blood flow and a system for converting fats to carbohydrates. A woman's estrogen hormone both makes her blood vessels more pliable than a man's and stimulates her liver to produce HDL more efficiently. Testosterone, on the other hand, causes men to have higher concentrations of the LDL that eventually clogs his arteries. With the onset of menopause and the accompanying decrease in estrogen, a woman's LDL catches up and sometimes surpasses that of a man's. But luckily for women their higher levels of HDL still leave them better protected than men.

THE TALE OF THE TAPE

Puberty has been described as an "awkward" age. Both sexes start growing upwards as well as outwards, and since girls start puberty earlier, we are often presented with the rather droll spectacle of girls towering over same-age boys at school dances. Much toe stepping and other embarrassments occur at these events. Physical growth is much more uneven or "jumpy" during puberty than it was previously, especially for boys. Bones grow faster than do the muscles attached to them, leading to a noticeable clumsiness as boys and girls try to adjust to the new lengths and forms of their appendages. All is well in the end, and physically the finished man and women end up resembling the measurements given in Figure 2.

Figure 2. The "Average" Man and Woman

	Men	Women
Height	5 feet 9 inches	5 feet 4 inches
Weight	165 pounds	135 pounds
Chest/Bust	39 inches	35 inches
Waist	32 inches	29 inches
Hips	38 inches	38 inches

Although the numbers in Figure 2 are from insurance statistics, the same source informs us that men typically report an average of one-half inch more than their actual height, and that the typical woman subtracts about five pounds from her weight. That would make the average man about 5'8½" and the average woman about 140 pounds.

Between the ages of twenty-five and seventy, the average man loses about two inches in height and the average woman about one and a half inches. Between the same ages the average man gains about twenty pounds and the average woman gains about twenty-five pounds. This a a natural and normal function of metabolic slowdown.

SIZING UP AND MONKEYING AROUND

So men are about 7 percent taller and 18 percent heavier than women. but is there any reason for this? Among the various primate species (the great ape order to which humans belong) we see quite a variety in height and weight differences between the sexes. Gibbons of both sexes are approximately the same height and weight, but male baboons are about 22 percent taller and 80 percent heavier than female baboons. If the same differences existed among humans and if we take the actual female average as the human standard, the average male would be 6'6" and weigh 243 pounds. If we take the actual male average as the human standard, the female would be 4'7" and weigh 92 pounds.

The differences in size among the various primates are related to the degree of promiscuity and monogamy among them. The more promiscuous the species the greater the size difference between the sexes. Baboons are the most promiscuous of the primates, gibbons the least, and humans somewhere in between. Gibbons stay with a single mate throughout life, and this one-to-one rule assures that male gibbons of all sizes have an equal chance to mate. The bawdy baboons engage in a ferocious scramble to impregnate as many females as they can during mating season. The biggest and strongest males are able to grab more than their fair share; the smallest and weakest perhaps enjoy no opportunity to mate at all. This mating scramble led to the evolutionary selection for greater size in the male baboon species, and to a greater and greater divergence in size between males and females.

Three-million-year-old fossils of our ancestors *Australophithecus afarensis* show that males were 20 percent taller and about twice as heavy as females back then. The fossil evidence for the human evolutionary tree shows a consistent decrease in the size difference between males and females. Perhaps it was our human cultural arrangements defining who had legitimate mating access to who that made us progressively less like baboons and more like gibbons.

SHEIKING THE FAMILY TREE AND PLAYING RUSSIAN ROULETTE

Speaking of mating and reproducing, there's obviously a vast difference in the reproductive potential between men and women. After all, a man can potentially father hundreds of offspring while a woman is pregnant with one. Men mate like baboons if they are able, but women would rather emulate the gibbon. Females reproduce at a fairly equal and constant rate, but there is a great deal more variability among the more competitive male. The extremes of this potential, reported in the *Guinness Book of World Records*. show that the male record, achieved by a nineteenth-century Arabic sheik with a bevy of wives, was an astonishing 888 offspring, give or take a few! The female record, even more astonishing given the greater female investment in reproduction, is 69. This was achieved by an eighteenth-century Russian woman who, in twenty-seven different confinements, gave birth to four sets of quadruplets, seven sets of triplets, and sixteen sets of twins. We feel that although many a man in a similar copulatory paradise would like to give the sheik a run for his money, the prospect of coming anywhere in the vicinity of the Russian's record would be any woman's worst nightmare.

PLAYING "HURRY UP AND WAIT"

"Jane!" exclaimed John in the direction of Jane, "We're gonna be late again! Why am I always waiting for you?" From getting ready to go to the in-laws to waiting for her to climax, it seems as though John is always waiting. When John gets ready to go out all dressed up, it takes him the male average time of about thirty minutes, including shower. Jane, like most of her sex, takes about fifty minutes.

Over a span of fifty years, assuming one "dressy" day each week, Jane will have spent about two years and four months longer than John getting ready. If she is married to John for twenty-five years, the poor man will have spent about a year of his life just waiting around for her to complete the finishing touches. It has been estimated that women use between seventeen and twenty-one different items (count 'em) for getting their bodies ready to go out. A male typically uses only about nine (hair brush and a hair groomer, toothbrush and toothpaste, razor, shaving cream, shaving lotion, soap, deodorant). No wonder women are about twice as likely as men to skip breakfast.

Men and women live out their lives, from cradle to grave, waiting for or catching up with members of the opposite sex. When John and Jane had their two children, Sally remained in Jane's womb one day longer than Mark. Nothing unusual about that though—on average, girl babies linger in the womb one day longer than boy babies (280 versus 279 days). When Sally did appear she had about a four- to six-week head start in her general maturity level over Mark at the same stage. She spoke a little earlier (and a little better) than Mark, but Mark started crawling and walking before her.

Females more than make up for that one lost day of life, as well as the two extra years spent preening. Jane can can expect to wait about 2,650 days to join John at eternal rest. She will do so when she is about 79 years old versus 72 for John.

RUNNING HOT AND COLD

Ever wonder how many marital spats have been caused by turning the thermostat up and down? We don't know the answer to that question, but we do know that men and women differ quite a bit in their tolerance for heat and cold. Women have more sweat glands per square inch of skin than men, but when the sweating begins it begins at lower temperatures than for men. Men's rate of sweating, especially in humid climates, is about 50 percent greater than women's. In hot and humid conditions a woman's skin temperature is about one degree warmer than a man's because she doesn't cool off by sweating as efficiently as a man, and so she is more prone to heat exhaustion. And, by the way, men sweat more heavily on their chests, women under their armpits.

Although it's usually a woman who wants to turn up the thermostat or throw that extra blanket on the bed, she is actually better able to tolerate cold than a man. She tends to have a thicker layer of fat than a man, and this is why most successful English Channel swimmers are women. Curiously though, women are significantly more likely to get frostbitten fingers and toes (areas with little fat on them) than men.

PUSHIN' AND PULLIN'

Women may be constitutionally stronger than men, but when it comes to specific feats of strength and endurance men are much stronger. This is not news to you; everybody knows that men are bigger, so they must be stronger. But there's more to strength than height and weight. If height and weight accounted for all the difference between the strength of the sexes, men would be only about 15 percent stronger rather than the actual average of about 40 percent stronger. In both sexes body weight accounts for only about one-third of the variation in strength, and height a mere 10 percent. This means that about 57 percent of the variation in strength among individuals is accounted for by factors other than height and weight.

It's mainly the ratio of muscle mass to non-muscle body weight that makes the difference. Large differences in muscle mass between girls and boys don't exist until about age thirteen, and neither do large strength differences. But when girls and boys reach puberty there is a marked change in physical abilities of the sexes. Male strength begins to increase appreciably with the onset of puberty, and may continue to age thirty-five. Female strength does not significantly increase at puberty in the same way; the average thirty-year-old female is not very much stronger than her fifteen-year-old sister.

The difference in strength between the sexes is mostly attributable to differences in sex hormone levels that are most noticeable at puberty. The male hormone testosterone is an anabolic (constructive) steroid that promotes the formation of muscle. The female hormone estrogen is a catabolic (destructive of protein) steroid that promotes the formation of fat. This is the reason that, on average, only 23 percent of a typical woman's bulk is in the form of muscle, while 28 percent of her body bulk is fat. For the typical man, 40 percent of his body bulk is muscle and only 15 percent is fat. So pound for pound he has about twice as much muscle as she, and she has about twice as much fat as he.

The arm strength of the average adult female is about 56 percent of that of the average male, and her leg strength is about 72 percent of the average male's. In overall strength female strength is 60 percent of male strength, but when adjustment is made for muscle mass she is 80 percent as strong.

Only 5 out of 140 women in a class at the U.S. Naval Academy were able to do more than one chin-up on entry. Males in the same class averaged 9 chin-ups. Female Middies were not so far off in the tummy area, however. They were able to do 90 percent of the male sit-ups average.

HUFFIN' AND PUFFIN'

The average man has a gallon and a half of blood coursing through his body; the average woman has four-fifths of a gallon. Not only does a man have more blood, he has about one million more blood cells in each drop of it than a woman does, which makes his blood thicker and faster to clot. But men manufacture blood less effectively than women.

The average woman's eight-ounce heart requires about seven more beats per minute to circulate her blood through her system than does the average man's ten-ounce heart. One observable result of this difference is the male's greater endurance, the capacity to expend energy over a period of time. What mostly determines endurance is something called *maximal oxygen uptake* (MOU). The MOU for the typical untrained young male of twenty-one is about 45 milliliters per kilogram of weight as opposed to about 33 milliliters per kilogram for an untrained women of the same age. The importance of sex hormones is once again underscored by the fact that there is no significant difference in MOU between the sexes until puberty.

Because women have less blood and about 15 percent less hemoglobin (an iron-containing protein in our blood cells that transports oxygen) than men, they have less oxygen available in their arterial blood, and thus generally less endurance. But that's not the whole story. Lung capacity (the ability to breathe in more air) is about 20 percent less in the average female than in the average male. Even adjusting for age and size, a woman's lung capacity is 10 percent less. The difference between the sexes in MOU lasts across the post-pubescent lifespan, with the MOU of the average sixty-five-year-old man being about the same as a twenty-five-year-old woman.

The most common kind of blood worldwide is type O. Men with type O blood live longer than men with type B blood; for females it is exactly the opposite. No one knows exactly why.

The normal adult pulse rate is 70 to 72 for men and 78 to 82 for women.

When women are touched they record an average drop in blood pressure. This indicates that their physiology perceives the touch as reassuring and nonthreatening. On the other hand, men experience an average *rise* in blood pressure on being touched, indicating that they perceive it as threatening, embarrassing, or possibly a sexual come-on.

Men tend to take deeper, longer breaths than women (an average of about 16 per minute), and to breath from the diaphragm. Women take shorter, shallower breaths (an average of about 22 per minute), and tend to breath from the upper part of the chest.

WE SHALL OVERCOME

A recent edition of the television show "A Current Affair" featured a sixty-three-year-old grandmother who bench presses 205 pounds! The average American male of college age bench presses only 146 pounds for one repetition (82 pounds for the average college age female). While this shows that a woman can increase her strength by serious weightlifting to the point that she is significantly stronger than the average male, the same amount of training performed by a male will see the male/female strength difference become even greater than it is between untrained men and women. Among the strongest male and female weight lifters, pound for pound, men are about twice as strong.

On the plus side, women lose less of their capacity to exercise as they get older. A sixty-year-old women has 90 percent of the capacity she had at age twenty; a sixty-year-old man has only 60 percent of the capacity he had at twenty. In terms of strength, the average sixty-five-year-old woman is 90 percent as strong as she was at thirty, but the sixty-five-year-old man is only 80 percent as strong as he was at thirty. Nevertheless, the male senior citizen remains significantly stronger than his female counterpart.

Women can also engage in aerobic exercise to the point where their performance substantially exceeds that of the average man. There are many women who can run the marathon, whereas Mr. Average gets winded running down a bus. But if an unfit Mr. and Ms. Average engage in exactly the same training schedule, the difference between them will be greater than it was when they were unfit. When they first start training he will pump about 100 milliliters of oxygenated blood with each heartbeat, she will pump about 75 for a difference of 25 milliliters. After a good period of training the difference between them in terms of blood pumped will have doubled, with he pumping about 160 milliliters and she about 110, a difference of 50 milliliters.

Women do better than men in super-stamina events such as long distance running and swimming—we're talking *really* long, ultramarathon distances. Mile for mile, men run and swim faster than women, but when certain thresholds are reached it is the well-trained female who more easily overcomes them. It is a rare trained female who experiences the extreme discomfort ("hitting the wall") reported by many males during a marathon race. And, as noted earlier, most swimmers of the English Channel are women.

The buoyancy and insulation provided by a female's greater supply of fat explains her sterling channel-swimming performance. Although the female marathon runner will have far less fat than her channel-swimming sister, she is better able to use her storage of fat to supply her energy needs than is a man. "Hitting the wall" happens to men when the glycogen available to their leg muscles runs dry. Glycogen is stored in the liver and skeletal muscle cells. When the body needs quick energy, it breaks glycogen down into glucose to provide it. A woman stores glycogen, as she stores fat and other sources of internal energy, more securely than a man and has more of it available when needed.

THAT'S STRETCHING IT A BIT

If you've ever watched children gyrating or gymnasts at work you will know that females are much more flexible than males. This extra flexibility is relited to a sex hormone called relaxin. Produced in greater quantities by women, this hormone softens, stretches, and relaxes the ligaments that attach muscles to bones. Its primary function is probably related to softening the pelvis for labor and birth.

A LITTLE RIBBING

About one woman out of every forty-two has an extra rib. One man in every fourteen has such a spare part. We don't know what to make of that, but it certainly does not mean that there's any truth to the story that Adam ribbed Eve into existence.

LET'S FACE IT

Have you ever wondered why among older married couples who are about the same age the man always seems visibly younger than his wife? Just think about George and Barbara Bush to get you started. According to dermatologists and plastic surgeons, although women age better than men physiologically, facially they age about ten years sooner. It may be true, as George Orwell wrote, that, "At age 50, every man has the face he deserves," but for women of the same age her mirror may be reflecting "cruel and unusual punishment."

Both men and women lose the elasticity of their skin as they age, but women lose it faster. We know we're talking about the face, but let's try a little experiment with the skin on the back of our hands. Try pinching the skin on the back of your hand for two seconds, let it go, and record the time the skin takes to flatten back out completely. If you are thirty or younger, man or woman, it will spring back instantly. In the forties, a man's skin will return to normal in one second, a woman's in three seconds. In the fifties, the respective male and female times are 4 and 12 seconds. So the elasticity of the average man's skin in his fifties is about the same as the average woman's in her forties.

This sorry state of affairs is attributable to a number of facts. Women have less facial substructure, thinner skin, and fewer hair follicles to hold the skin in place. A woman's delicate, sensitive, and hairless face, considered such a boon in the prime of her youth, turns traitor on her later in life to become a bane. A woman's thinner skin also provides less protection from the sun, leading to more wrinkles per hour of sun exposure for her than for him. The fact that men shave their faces also helps because shaving increases blood flow to the face and removes dead skin cells, thus increasing the rate of rejuvenation.

Researchers at the University of California at San Diego have found out that regular aerobic activity can significantly slow down skin-cell aging. Exercise carries blood, oxygen, and other nutrients to deep skin cells, making them thicker, healthier, and more resilient. Exercise may also increase testosterone levels in both sexes. Increased testosterone—in addition to having a healthy effect on the libido—may help to retard aging because it increases the cell's ability to absorb rebuilding protein.

Women appear to have discovered the benefits of exercise and are doing it about as much as men these days. According to a National Sporting Goods Association survey, women outnumber men in aerobics, exercise walking, swimming, and bicycling. Men remain in the lead in team sports, weightlifting, and running, and the "macho" sports like boxing and wrestling remain almost exclusively male domains. But 53 percent of those who work out in health clubs are women.

"Vanity, thy name is woman," wrote some ancient misogynist. How true this is you can judge for yourself. Of the 183 face-lifts performed every day in the United States, women have 90 percent. Of the 225 nose jobs performed every day, women have 75 percent.

One survey taker reports that eight of ten eleven-year-old girls nationwide think that they're overweight, compared with one out of ten eleven-year-old boys. Because the fat layering effects of puberty have had little effect on girls by this age it is unlikely that there is a large objective difference in obesity between the sexes at this time.

Of the 101 million Americans who are on diets at any given time, 59 percent are female. Women take their dieting more seriously than men, with over 90 percent of Weight Watchers members and 75 percent of Nutri/System customers being women. Sometimes the quest for "a slimmer you" is taken far too seriously. About 93 percent of recorded cases of anorexia nervosa (a compulsive drive for thinness leading to a disgust for food) are female. Women are also more likely to turn to diet pills; about 88 percent of the users of these products are women.

According to one survey, 47 percent of men and 31 percent of women sleep in their birthday suits. This difference might be explained by another survey finding: 68 percent of the men said that when they posed naked they liked what they saw in the mirror; only 22 percent of the women liked the way they looked *au naturel.*

HAIR TODAY GONE TOMORROW

Men and women have the same number of body hairs per square inch of skin, but a woman's hairs are not as noticeable as a man's because her hair is thinner and less densely colored, much like the peach fuzz of prepubescent boys. Apart from the genitals, hair growth patterns are the most visible of the physical features that distinguish males from females. In fact, we take pains to maximize differences between ourselves and the opposite sex in the hair department. In general, women let their head hair grow, men don't; women pluck their eyebrows and elongate their eyelashes, men don't; women shave their armpits and legs, men don't. Men grow moustaches and beards, most women thankfully cannot.

A woman experiences a thinning of her scalp and pubic hair as she ages, but a man actually gets hairier. Unfortunately, this hair tends to accumulate on the back and inside the nose and ears, which is hardly just compensation for the loss of his crowning glory. Men lose about a hundred hairs a day on the scalp, as do women, but most of a woman's hair grows back. Because of the influence of testosterone, most men eventually lose the greater proportion of their scalp hair. Believe it or not, the receding of the male hairline begins at puberty.

Have you ever heard of trichotillomania? It is a strange compulsion that causes sufferers, about 90 percent of whom are women, to pull out their hair. These women pull out hair, strand by strand, sometimes to the point of baldness, and some even pull hair from eyebrows and lashes, and arm, leg, and pubic hair. No one knows for sure why this hairy predicament is overwhelmingly a female compulsion. But because the affliction can be controlled by certain antidepressant drugs, and because women are more prone to depression, the disorder may be linked to the sex hormones.

Men's and women's hair grays at the same rate, but 40 percent of graying women versus 8 percent of graying men use dyes to cover the gray.

THE NOSE KNOWS

Even after making adjustments for body size, males have larger noses than females. Since ancient times the nose has been considered a phallic symbol. The nose, as well as the penis, becomes engorged with blood when its owner is sexually aroused. Although hardly anyone notices it, both appendages become swollen, warmer, and more sensitive. Perhaps there's some rhyme and reason to the custom of rubbing noses after all.

Women, particularly those of child-bearing age, have a much keener sense of smell than men. The female hormone estrogen is a major activator of the olfactory (smell) receptors, and the smell she is best able to detect is the musky odor of the male body. During the ovulation period of her cycle (that's when estrogen levels peak) a woman can detect musk anywhere between 100 and 10,000 times more clearly than during menstruation, when estrogen levels are at their lowest. Also, on average, her ability to detect this particular odor is a 1,000 times better than a man's. Women's sense of smell deteriorates much more slowly than does a man's.

Male body odor is stronger than female body odor because male sweating starts at a lower temperature and is more copious. Another reason is that his hairier body is able to play host to more bacteria that smell as they decay. Because men's sense of smell is less keen than women's, many men remain blissfully ignorant of their odor.

Women don't have keener smell receptors than men to smell the coffee. The traits that we possess in greater or lesser quantities all have an evolutionary history of usefulness. Take the series of studies done in Glasgow, Scotland, showing that about 80 percent of new mothers could recognize their infants by smell alone. This may have had survival benefits eons ago as mothers went about their nurturing tasks in dark, dank caves. No new father in these studies was able to do this.

WHAT? ME SNORE?

About one-third of all males over thirty snore; snoring men outnumber snoring women by about twenty to one. Snoring is a vibration caused by partial obstruction of the throat brought on by sleep-relaxed muscles. No one really knows the why's behind this difference, but because most snoring women are postmenopausal, sex hormone influences (primarily progesteron :) are once again suspected. We know that women are lighter sleepers than males, suffer more insomnia (about twice as many females than males take sleeping pills on a fairly regular basis), and are more easily awakened by baby's crying. It may be that females relax less during sleep while in their child-rearing years precisely because they have to be aware of and sensitive to baby's needs at all times. After menopause, a woman's changing sex hormone balance may allow for more relaxed sleep—and more snoring. In fact, Just about as many postmenopausal women as men snore.

LIP SERVICE

Female lips are more everted—rolled back to expose some of the mucous membrane of the mouth—than male lips. No other primate has everted lips. For thousands of years women have shown a desire to emphasize the size and coloring of their lips by painting them. With the exception of some ceremonial lip-painting, in no known culture has the heterosexual male felt the need to paint his lips. It has been suggested that evolution everted female lips more strongly to mimic the lips of the vagina so that sexual receptiveness could be signaled by them. Lip signaling took the place of genital signaling due to the human female's loss of estrus ("heat"), and the more hidden positioning of the vagina that accompanied the evolution of the human upright stance.

Since we're talking about lips, we might point out that females use them significantly more often to smile than do men (check this out with your high school yearbooks). This difference is noted from early infancy to late adulthood, and is probably partly innate. We can say this because we observe significantly greater reflexive (non-learned) smiling in female infants than in male infants. Reflexive smiling occurs in about the first six weeks of life before behavior control is transferred from parts of the brain responsible for automatic (reflexive) responses to parts of the brain responsible for learned behavior. Since behavior during this period is unlearned, the smile is unlearned.

Although women smile more often, a study conducted with children indicated that a smile and a friendly word from a man was seen by these children as more positive. Apparently, because women smile more often the message conveyed by it is less clear to children than is the message conveyed by a man. In most areas of life, the rarer something is the more it is valued.

THE EYES HAVE IT

Proportional to body size, women have slightly larger eyes than men. They also have a higher proportion of white than men, and that, along with the artificial enhancement produced by eye shadow and mascara, makes female eyes seem bigger than they actually are. Needless to say, men find large feminine eyes to be very attractive. Women tend to find smaller eyes more attractive in men.

Niney-nine percent of all cases of color blindness occur in men. Like hemophilia, color blindness is a sex-linked trait—females carry the recessive genes for it, but it is generally expressed only in males. Those few women who do suffer from color blindness are daughters of a carrier mother and a color blind father, a very rare combination.

Although men like to joke about "women drivers," insurance companies know that women are safer drivers than men and reward them for being so with smaller premiums. Motor vehicle accident death rates are about 2.4 times higher for men (28.8 per 100,000) than for women (11.9 per 100,000). Even when you take the fact that men drive more often than women into account, it still remains true that men have twice as many fatal accidents per miles driven as women.

There are a variety of reasons why men have more accidents than women: they drink and drive more often, they drive faster and more aggressively, they are less likely to signal a turn and more likely to try to "beat the light." But another part of the answer could be the slight differences in how men and women see. Men have more sensitive cones in their eyes than women, enabling them to see better in bright light; women have more sensitive rods than men, enabling them to see better in the dark. Women's eyes are also sensitive to red.

We don't think that these small differences mean that a disproportionate number of accidents involving male drivers occur because men fail to see the red stop-light at night. Perhaps women are more careful than men because they fear that if they get into an accident the newspapers may print their age.

Although men have a better sense of visual perspective than women, it tends to be more "tunneled." Women have a greater number of cones and receptor rods in the retina, giving them a wider arc of vision. As a result a woman's peripheral vision is better than a man's—she can see objects coming at her from the rear and side sooner than a man. This, in conjunction with the other factors mentioned, contribute to the lower accident rate for female drivers.

Despite the fact that women are more reluctant to wear corrective lenses, there are about 11 million more women than men in the United States who wear them (43 million men versus 54 million women). Eyesight is the only sense in which, generally speaking, men show superiority over women.

SPEAKING UP (AND DOWN)

Men's voices are pitched lower than women's and have a shorter range (three tones to the woman's five). Because we can detect higher-pitched sounds better than lower ones, despite a man's louder voice we can actually hear a woman's voice further away (a maximum of about 220 yards) than we can a man's (a maximum of about 200 yards).

Differences are not really pronounced until puberty, at which time the male voice "breaks" (deepens) under the influence of testosterone. The deeper the voice the more testosterone the chap has (studies have shown that basses have more ejaculations than tenors). The female retains a more childlike pitch of between 230 and 250 cycles per second while the male's dips at puberty and onwards to between 130 and 140. The male voice becomes even less flexible with age, as does the voice of the postmeno-pausal woman.

An outward sign of the male's deepening voice is his Adam's apple, which is about 30 percent larger than a woman's. In fact, you will hardly ever see a woman with a prominent Adam's apple; if you do the odds are that "she" is a man in drag. The male's vocal cords in his voice box are longer (about 18 millimeters) than a woman's (about 13 millimeters).

For some unknown reason, but again probably related to hormonal imbalance related to the occupation (frequent surges of testosterone per-haps?), long-term prostitutes develop a larger larynx (set of vocal chords) and a deeper voice than other women. This gives a whole new meaning to the term "deep throat."

Those same Glasgow studies mentioned earlier also found that about 80 percent of new mothers could distinguish their infants' cries from among a number of other infants' cries. Again, no new fathers were able to do this.

3

Brains, Minds, and Abilities

SEX ON THE BRAIN

Everybody has sex on the brains even the Puritans among us. We don't mean that we slink around all day with leering smiles, lost in sexual fantasy, or that our gonads are forever on go. We mean that men and women are different because our brains are different; they are constructed differently and they process information differently. There are vastly more similarities between male and female brains than there are differences, but it is those differences that most excite us, provide us with different perceptions and priorities, and lead us to behave differently. Men speak a physical language, they are seers and doers with little patience for impracticality and foo foo. They're always seeking faster ways to get more, better, different. Women speak a more emotional and spiritual language; they love impracticality and foo foo. Women also like more, better and different, but they are not driven to get it and they appreciate better what they have.

SEX AT THE MALL

Check out the male and female shoppers at the local mall. The ladies are having a lolly time a choosin' and a chattin'; their menfolk sulk along behind them wondering what in the hell they're doing there again and swearing never to return. When Dick just has to buy something he goes out and does it; shopping is the unfortunate means he must employ to meet this end. Jane enjoys shopping for its own sake; buying makes it that much better. When Dick buys something he is mostly interested in function and durability; if it also looks good, well, that's great too. Jane also likes function and durability, but it must first and foremost look nice, be pretty, and match something or other. The typical woman will take just over twice as long as the typical man to make up her mind when purchasing most sex-neutral items; she will take over three times as long her selecting personal apparel than will a man selecting his.

We might say that sex differences in shopping and buying are learned, but we believe that the legacy of our evolutionary past is staring us in the face at the mall. For about 99.9 percent of our species' history the basic division of labor was man the hunter and woman the gatherer. When Urk the caveman went hunting scarce prey he had to take the first game he came across. He had no time to appraise it, and it mattered not one whit if it had fine feathers or was otherwise beautiful; if it moved it was meat, period. Urk needed a brain that favored quick perception and selection, the ability to judge distances, and good coordination between eye and hand; in short, he needed visual/spatial skills. If he dillydallied assessing the succulent possibilities of his prey or how nice it would look on the spit, he ran the danger of losing it, or maybe ending up the dinner instead of the diner.

His cave mate, Moog, had the more leisurely and less dangerous task of gathering from the land. She had the time to examine and pick the ripest berries, the fattest fruits, and had to discriminate among a variety

of tastes and textures. She did this in the company of other women with whom she could discuss at length the finer points of each choice and how best it could be prepared. Unlike Urk, she *had* to be finicky; the wrong roots and herbs can kill you just as surely, if less messily, than the game that Urk hunted. The more she took time to talk with and listen to her sister gatherers, the more she honed her communication and shopping skills. Failure to properly evaluate the variety of goodies available to her may have earned her a bop over the head from Urk, who didn't at all mind being called a chauvinist pig. Thus evolution favored rapid no-nonsense hunting for males and careful selective gathering for females—which is exactly what we see at the mall today.

Sure, we hunt and gather at the grocery store today, and our meats, fruits, cereals, and veggies have been killed, gutted, peeled, sanitized, packaged, and frozen long before we get there, but we're still a bunch of Urks and Moogs upstairs. Our evolutionary history has left lasting impressions on the human brain that are visible at the mall. These histories involved not only feeding but also fleeing, fighting, and that other thing—you know, the fourth F. Male and female brains became sex-differentiated according to the roles they had to play over the eons of evolutionary time that formed us. Before we look at other mental differences we have to look at the organ that makes them possible.

FROM FEMALE TO MALE: THE BRAIN DRAIN

The human brain is about the size of a large grapefruit and looks something like a walnut-shaped blob of gray Jell-o. The average man's brain measures 87.4 cubic inches; the average woman's measures 76.8 cubic inches. This difference doesn't mean that men are smarter than women; a woman's brain is a tiny bit larger than a man's after adjustment is made for body size. Despite its small size and unassuming appearance, the brain is the most wondrous and complicated structure in the known universe. It operates as a kind of giant relay system sending messages by electrical and chemical impulses from brain cell to brain cell. Although no one has yet heard from the Almighty how many there really are, various estimates of the number of communicating cells in our brains (we call them neurons) range between 10 billion and 100 billion. Each of these billions of neurons can make perhaps as many as 4,000 connections—all communicating something or other—with other neurons. This gives us all an extraordinary degree of information potential. It has been estimated that the number of potential brain connections is about a hundred times more than the total number of connections made by all the telephone systems in the world on any given day!

We examined the genetic/hormonal stages of bodily sex differentiation earlier; the third stage is the sexing of the brain. Men and women not only look different because of what went on before birth, but are also predisposed to think and behave differently for the same reasons. We can all tell the difference between male and female plumbing, but it would take a brain anatomist to distinguish between male and female brains of equal size. There are slight differences in structure and functioning that influence responses to various situations in typical male or female directions. Just as the reproductive system of the fetus is female unless influenced by male hormones, the human brain will also develop in the female direction unless it is influenced by male hormones (remember those XY folks with the androgen insensitivity syndrome?).

To make a very long and complicated story as short and simple as possible, after the male testes are formed they begin to secrete androgens. Between six and eight weeks after conception, the XY fetal brain receives genetic instructions telling it that it is time for a very important bath. The faucet is turned on, and out pours sufficient male hormones to change the brain from the basic female pattern to the male pattern. This so-called "androgen bath" makes certain parts of the brain sensitive thereafter to the effects of testosterone. When a male reaches puberty, testosterone activates his brain to engage in male-typical behavior, especially male-typical sexual and aggressive behavior. The female brain has a much gentler, though more complicated pattern.

Just as we get to talk to different people when we dial different numbers on the telephone, important sex differences in behavior and emotion occur because of the different paths these connections travel in male and female brains. The chief administrative operator determining what brain trails incoming information will travel along is a pea-sized brain structure called the hypothalamus. The hypothalamus controls our basic survival functions; it synthesizes hormones, regulates body temperature, eating, drinking, sexual behavior and emotions, among other things. If male hormones bathe the hypothalamus at the critical period of fetal development, it will settle into the male rhythm of hormone secretion. If not, it will settle into the more complicated female rhythm. This isn't an all-or-nothing process; some brains are more masculinized than others, and sometimes we dial the wrong number.

The preoptic area of the hypothalamus is larger in females than in males, and, more importantly, the neuronal connections in this area are "wired" differently in the two sexes. Even when both sexes receive a surge of the same hormone—say testosterone—the female brain "feminizes" it by changing it into a hormone called estradiol, the major estrogen. Estradiol promotes nurturing behavior in females by lowering the threshold for the activation of neurons in the preoptic area. The male preoptic area does not respond to estradiol, nor the female preoptic to testosterone. In the male brain, testosterone lowers the threshold for activating the amygdal, the area of the brain most associated with aggression and violence.

Recent research has also shown that a certain cluster of cells in the part of the brain that regulates sexual behavior, called the anterior hypothalamus, is twice as large in heterosexual males as it is in heterosexual females. Because the same cell size difference is also found between hetersexual and homosexual males, it appears that this area may regulate the targets of our sexual urges rather than their strength.

Having not been sensitized to androgen at the fetal stage, the female brain is less receptive to it in later life. Even if she were, she will secrete less of it to be sensitive to. Both sexes secrete testosterone, but post-pubescent males secrete about fifteen times more than post-pubescent females. Females secrete ten times more progesterone (the "nurturing" hormone) than males. It is thought that progesterone protects the female fetus from the effects of what testosterone there is floating about in her brain. Remember, the basic human brain is female, so there is no such thing as a "progesterone bath" necessary to feminize the XX brain. Progesterone serves simply to protect what already exists from the diverting influence of testosterone. Many of the sex differences outlined in this book can be traced directly or indirectly to these and other differences in brain organization laid down in early development.

WOMEN: THE SCATTERBRAINED SEX

So sex hormones "pre-wire" our brains along sex-typical lines while still in the womb, and this pre-wiring leaves a lasting imprint on brain organization. But this isn't the whole story. It's a matter of modern folklore that the brain consists of two separate but interacting "hemispheres" joined at the center by a bridge called the corpus callosum ("hard body"). Although the hemispheres work as a team like two lumberjacks at different ends of a saw, each controls different things (although there is much overlap). The left side is practical, rational, and concrete, and it controls our verbal skills; the right side is emotional and abstract, and controls our visual and spatial abilities. The left side of the brain controls the right side of the body, and the right side of the brain the left side of the body.

A man's brain is more specialized or "lateralized" than a woman's, meaning that his abilities are more exclusively controlled by the side of the brain most strongly organized for those abilities. For instance, if Dick is working on an abstract problem, measures of electrical brain activity show that he is almost exclusively operating from the right hemisphere, but when he talks about the problem he switches operations to the speech centers on the left. When Jane is working on the same problem she uses both sides of her brain at the same time regardless of whether she is thinking about it or talking about it.

Brain scientists believe that this superior female hemispheric integration is probably due in part to the fact that she has a significantly thicker splenium than a male. The splenium is a bundle of fibers that compose the rear fifth of the corpus callosum, and recent research has shown that females have a few hundred thousand more of these communicating fibers in their splenia. Just as more cables in a telephone system means that more people are hooked up to it and can communicate with other subscribers through it, the additional fibers in the female brain means that there is a greater level of communication between her two hemispheres. The old saw that declared that, "It is a woman's prerogative to change her mind," had more truth to it than we suspected.

The lesser degree of specialization of the female brain, or if you like, its greater ability to "change its mind," has many positive advantages. Women recover from strokes and other brain injuries much faster and more completely than males because the functions of the injured area of one hemisphere are more readily transferred to the other. A woman's more integrated brain may also account for the fact that there are many more cases of brain developmental disorders such as aphasia, dyslexia, and autism among males than among females. So the next time some man calls you a scatterbrain, Ms., take it as a compliment.

HOW DID YOU KNOW THAT?

Many of us equate "woman's intuition" with weird paranormal phenomena operating outside the normal channels of our senses, and therefore want to trash the whole idea. Others marvel at the remarkable ability of many women to know when something's amiss or their ability to get to the "heart of the matter." There is nothing really weird or "extrasensory" about it; it's just that a woman's senses are sharper and more refined than a man's, especially in matters of the heart. One of the reasons for this lies in a little brain mechanism called the reticular activating system (RAS). The RAS is a bundle of neurons in the upper part of the brain stem that monitors all incoming stimulation; it is the gatekeeper of alertness and attention. If incoming stimulation is sufficiently novel and/or intense, the RAS generates enough chemical activity to pass it on to the higher brain centers for interpretation and response; if it is routine and/ or mild, it will not. The same stimulus that is intense and meaningful for some of us is routine and for others. Some folks need intense stimulation to goad the RAS into paying attention and passing the stimulus on; others require very little. Psychologists call the former stimuli *reducers* and the latter stimuli *augmenters*. These names refer to RAS functioning, not to any conscious or purposeful property of individuals.

Many brain chemicals contribute to the RAS, either reducing or exaggerating the meaningfulness of incoming information, with most of them being influenced by male androgens. As we have seen, females are more sensitive to touch, odors, and sounds, and, as we shall see later, they are also more sensitive to emotion. So, as we would expect, brain wave patterns tracing RAS arousal to other brain centers show a strong tendency for females to be augmenters and for males to be reducers. Men also have a stronger tendency to have RASs that more quickly get used to various kinds of stimulation, and thus to pay less attention to them than they once did.

Female intuition may be no more mysterious than the alliance of her augmenting RAS with her splenium's superior switching gear. The female RAS pulls in sensory information from the environment that the male RAS may not attend to, so the woman has more "bits" of information available to her. Her splenium allows her to shunt those bits back and forth across her two hemispheres more efficiently than a man until she makes sense of them. Men tend to keep emotional information "in its place," which means the right side of the brain. Women have a greater ability to integrate emotional experiences felt in their right brains with their thinking, verbal left brains. This gives them the ability to be more in tune with the "felt life" of others and to "intuit" how they are feeling.

ANYTHING YOU CAN DO I CAN DO BETTER

Sex differences in brain structure lead to sex-based differences in various mental abilities. Generally speaking, men are superior in visual/spatial skills (quick perception of the shape of things and the space they occupy), just the kinds of skills Urk needed to get his supper. These are right hemisphere skills, and the cerebral cortex "rind" (the intricate layer of folded nerve cells that are the brain's "gray matter") covering the right hemisphere is thicker in males than in females. Females show a clear superiority over males in verbal skills, and the rind covering the left hemisphere is thicker in females. So both sexes are "thick-headed"—at least on one side.

Language processing occurs predominantly in the left hemisphere of the brain in both sexes. Despite the greater female scatter across the brain hemispheres, their language centers within the left hemisphere are more concentrated in the front area than they are among males. In men they are scattered more or less equally in the front and back of the left hemisphere, which makes it harder for males to acquire the rules of spelling, grammar, and writing. What does this mean in terms of intellectual abilities?

The most popular IQ tests used today are those developed by David Wechsler. The various Wechsler tests consist of two subtests assessing verbal and visual/spatial skills; the verbal IQ (VIQ) test measures verbal skills and the performance IQ (PIQ) test measures visual/spatial skills. Your overall "full-scale" IQ is obtained by adding your scores on both subtests and dividing by two. For instance, if you score 110 on PIQ and 90 on VIQ you would have a full-scale IQ of 100 ([110 + 90]/2 = 100). Brain scan tests show that the right side of the brain is most active when working on a PIQ item and the left side most active when working on a UIQ item.

Early versions of the Wechsler tests showed consistently large subscale differences between males and females; males scored significantly higher on PIQ and females scored significantly higher on VIQ. Neat! Now we had a test confirming what we always knew—men and women think differently. But Wechsler considered this a damn nuisance; after all, he was looking for an accurate measure of intelligence, not sex differences. To eliminate the nuisance, he fiddled around with the tests and eliminated items most strongly favoring one sex or the other until he arrived at a "sex neutral" IQ test.

Because of all this fudging, standard IQ tests no longer discriminate between the sexes on verbal and visual/spatial skills, but many other tests and observations do. Men almost always show clear superiority on maze running, eye/hand coordinaticn skills and on the math section of various tests such as the ACT, SAT, and GRE tests (math is very much a visual/spatial skill, especially trigonometry and geometry). One study conducted at Johns Hopkins University among boys and girls in the top 3 percent of the population on IQ found that boys were overrepresented by a ratio of thirteen to one at the top levels of the SAT math scores. The funny thing about this, though, is that girls get better average grades in math at almost all levels. This must mean that just as many boys do very poorly as boys who do very well, a situation that has the effect of making the boys' average a little lower than the girls'. Male/female differences at the upper extremes become more pronounced with the hormonal surges of puberty. Even among the severely retarded, male mathematical "idiot savants" outnumber females by five to one.

On the other hand, females almost always show clear superiority on the verbal sections of these tests (although these tests have been neutered as much as possible also). Females acquire language skills earlier and better because of the slight retarding effect of androgens on the left side of the male brain during brain sexual differentiation. There is only one girl for every four boys in remedial reading classes, and verbal disabilities such as stuttering and dyslexia occur four to ten times more often in boys than in girls.

WHAT'S UP, DOC?

These differing abilities shape the occupations we enjoy and seek. Have you noticed that many of the psychologists on the talk shows are women, but when it comes to interviewing the technical boffins they are almost all men? A survey of all 476,300 doctoral-level scientists (PhDs) living in the United States conducted by the National Institute of Science found that the sexes sorted themselves occupationally more or less according to their innate abilities. Males really dominated in the fields making most use of visual/spatial skills, with 97.4 percent of the engineers, 95.7 percent of the physicists, and 89.9 percent of the mathematicians being male. Women were much more represented in the "verbal" sciences. Psychology had the most female PhDs with 36 percent, followed by the medical sciences (31.7 percent) and the social sciences (22.7 percent).

There were more male than female scientists (82.7 to 17.3 percent), so this has to be taken into account. If there were no connection between sex and the scientific field chosen we would find each field to have about the same percentage of women in it as there are total female scientists; that is, 17.3 percent. By dividing the actual percentage of women in each science by the total percentage of female scientists, we find that female scientists are underrepresented by a factor 6.6 in engineering, 4.0 in physics, and 1.7 in math; they are overrepresented by a factor of 2.1 in psychology, 1.8 in the medical sciences, and 1.3 in the social sciences.

CLICKER POWER

Who wears the pants in your house? Never mind any other indicator, the true litmus test of sovereignty in the American castle is, "Who holds the television zapper?" Men's brains make them impatient, impulsive seekers after more and different, and they click their way though channels 1 to 40 and beyond to find it every time a commercial intrudes. The speed with which he changes channels produces little more than flashcards— 5 seconds of ice fishing, 8 seconds of wrestling, 2 seconds of opera— but the important thing is that he's *doing something* rather than passively waiting while the Madison Avenue wizards try to sell him the good life.

A woman watching TV by herself usually selects her program and sticks with it, even through the commercials. She may use the time to reflect on what she has been watching, or she may even tune into the ads. But if she is watching with her mate she has to endure his visual roller coaster, because in more than 90 percent of American households it is the man who enjoys the remote "control." It may be that the Mitachi 25 has bumped the Colt .45 as America's phallic symbol, at least for the couch potato set. Should a man lose control of the clicker—his toy and his tool—he may feel emasculated, literally out of control and "de-tooled." Sex-differentiated television watching is life in microcosm: men play the field, women seek commitment. Perhaps on the back of every man's armchair should be the warning. "You'll have to pry my zapper from my cold, dead hands." Click.

MOTHER NATURE MESSES MORE WITH MEN

Males and females consistently show the same IQ average (100), but the range of. IQ scores—the "spread" between the lowest and highest score—is much greater for males. Charles Darwin noted this greater range of intelligence long before the IQ test came along when he wrote: "there is greater variability in the male sex." Consider the male and female IQ distributions shown in Figure 3. Both sexes have the same average, but there are more females clustered around the middle and more males on both the low and high sides (much the same pattern exists with math scores). This means we will find both more geniuses and more idiots among males than among females. Despite this, it so happens that the two highest IQs ever reported were both attained by females, both of whom had scores over 200. We should also keep in mind that there is more variability *within* each sex than there is *between* them.

This greater spread or variability in males is not confined to IQ; there is a greater tendency toward extremes and abnormalities of all kinds in males. Even among identical twins there is greater variability on all sorts of traits among males than females. But why this greater variability (another name for "departure from the norm") among males? Recall that the female is the standard "unmodified" human being, and that it is the Y chromosome that modifies the standard form. We have seen how the second X chromosome protects women from many genetic diseases, and how her more "balanced" brain protects her from many developmental disorders. The activities of the Y chromosome and of the male hormones on the brain represent modifications of the standard human model. Trait extremes, either good or bad, represent the influence of these modifications. The species cannot afford severe departures from the norm among women. Their reproductive services are just too valuable. Males are much more "expendable" in reproductive terms, so nature can tinker with them more, adding a little here, taking away a little there.

We saw in chapter 1 that brain sexing is rarely an "all or nothing" matter. Brain sexing involves the operation of androgens on the right side of the brain, an operation that in males takes a little from the development of the left hemisphere and gives a little to the right hemisphere. Turner's syndrome women get little or no androgen, so their right brain hemisphere functioning is very poor relative to their left brain functioning. Their visual/spatial skills are so poor that they are often said to suffer from "space-form blindness." Their average verbal IQ is average to above average,

Figure 3. Average IQ, Male and Female

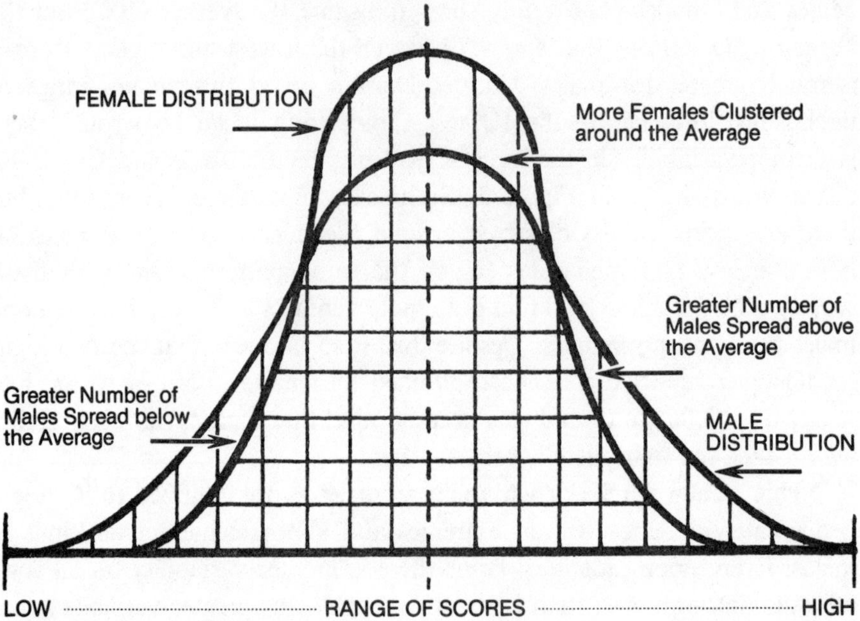

FEMALE DISTRIBUTION

More Females Clustered around the Average

Greater Number of Males Spread above the Average

Greater Number of Males Spread below the Average

MALE DISTRIBUTION

LOW ——————— RANGE OF SCORES ——————— HIGH

but their performance IQ is significantly below average. Androgen-insensitive genetic males also show poor visual/spatial skills.

On the other hand, congenital adrenal hyperplasia females, those who got more fetal androgens than normal for females, do very well on visual/spatial tasks, often surpassing the male average. Hormonally normal women also show much improved visual/spatial skills during phases of their menstrual cycles in which the female hormones are low and testosterone is relatively high. Oddly enough, XYY "supermales" do not show enhanced visual/spatial skills, and they usually score significantly below normal male averages in both verbal and performance IQ tests, although their performance IQ usually exceeds their verbal IQ.

YO! ARE YOU LISTENING?

Because of the relative dominance of the left hemisphere female babies, on average, start to talk about four months earlier than male babies—and then they never stop! Men of many different cultures have made half-serious jokes about their women's wagging tongues: "Where there's a women, there's no silence," exclaims the frazzled Frenchman; "The tongue is the sword of a woman, and she never lets it get rusty," chimes in the Chinaman; and the dour Scotsman perhaps takes a good thing further than most when he moans that "The North Sea will sooner be found wanting in water than a woman at a loss for a word. " But women are hitting back at their tongue-tied menfolk. Says the suffering Jewish wife: "Our ancestors wandered in the desert for forty years because, even in ancient times, men wouldn't stop to ask for directions."

At all ages, females talk more often than males. Women initiate spousal conversation three times more often than men. They not only speak more often, they also speak faster. The average women speaks 150 words a minute; the average male, 120. Let's see how this works out over ten years of marriage. Research shows that the typical married couple talk to each other ninety minutes per week, with the wife talking for sixty minutes, and the husband mumbling his replies for thirty minutes. That works out to:

Wife: 60 minutes per week at 150 words per minute = 9,000 words
Husband: 30 minutes per week at 120 words per minute = 3,600 words

In ten years:

Wife: = 52 × 9,000 (= 468,000) × 10 = 4,680,000
Husband: = 52 × 3,600 (= 187,200) × 10 = 1,872,000

Excess of women's words: = 2,808,000 words

Those 2 808,000 words represent about twenty average-sized books. But then, marriage counselors say that husbands listen to only about a quarter of what their wives say, and wives listen to only about half of what their husbands say. This means that husbands pay attention to about 1,170,000 of their wives' words, women to about 936,000 of their husbands' words. The up side to this is that the house is one of the few places you can talk uninterrupted—because people are hardly ever listening. In fact, "not listening" is the number-one complaint that most wives have about their husbands, and "never shutting up" is the number-one complaint that most husbands have against their wives.

It has been said that the typical American housewife has an average of 100 little worries on her mind every day, her husband an average of

55. No wonder she talks more often, but what in the world are both sexes so worried about? Men worry more about external things such as their work and achievements. Women, even if they work outside the home, worry more about interpersonal things such as family relationships and if they are pleasing other people.

Experiments tracing blood flow through the brain during language tests find interesting sex differences in the way the brain works. In both sexes, of course, the brain must work to understand the language and to control the responses of the vocal cords, jaw, tongue, and so forth. The blood flow "fit" between brain areas specialized for these activities and their expression is tight in male brains. There is a much looser fit in female brains, and strong blood flow is observed in the right as well as the left hemisphere. Cecille Naylor's research in this area leads her to say that it is as though women's brains are "ablaze" when processing language as they bring additional imaging functions and expanded emotional components to the business of processing language.

WHAT DO THEY TALK ABOUT?

When women get together the most popular topics of conversation are (1) illness, (2) children, (3) husbands, (4) other women, (5) clothes, (6) housework, (7) in-laws, (8) men, and (9) domestic activities such as sewing and cooking. Personal finances is the least discussed topic for women, closely followed by politics and religion. There is far more self-disclosure in woman-to-woman talk than in man-to-man talk.

Man-to-man conversation tends to center around (1) work, (2) sports and recreation, (3) sex, (4) automobiles and other machines, (5) current affairs (we assume that this means current political affairs), and (6) other men. For men, the least discussed topic is the body (their own bodies, that is).

When men and women talk to each other women tend to adapt their topics to the interests of males, with recreation/sports being the main topic, followed by work and money, and themselves. In mixed-sex groups, men tend to reverse their one-on-one reticence and talk more than women. Men are also three times more likely to interrupt women during a conversation than women are to interrupt men.

OH, FIDDLE-FADDLE!

No feature of spoken English is used only by one sex or the other, but certainly women are more circumspect: she goes to the restroom to "powder my nose," he goes to "shake the snake." Men are more ready to invent and use new terms, puns, slang, sexual double entendre, profanity, and obscenity, while some women wouldn't use the "S" word even if they had a mouthful. Teenage girls are an exception to this rule, but they mature out of it as they gain confidence and realize that swearing doesn't really make them "one of the boys." One magazine survey found that 66 percent of teenage boys were "put off" by girls who swore, but only 29 percent of the girls were likewise upset with boys who did. When women use swear words (and unfortunately more of them are doing so these days), they tend to do so at higher levels of provocation than men.

According to a team of University of Pennsylvania researchers, men lose their verbal abilities faster than women. Atrophy of the left hemishpere of the brain occurs two to three times faster in men. The mental integration skills decline about three times faster in men than in women as the corpus callosum gets progressively smaller with age. The researchers suggest that female hormones protect women's brains from cell loss, but we wonder if the old saying "use it or lose it" applies here also.

According to Ma Bell, women initiate two-thirds of all non-business telephone conversations.

OF ALL THE THINGS I'VE LOST, I MISS MY MIND THE MOST

I suppose we're all a bit wacky from time to time. One review of twenty-seven prevalence-rate studies conducted in North America and Europe found that about one in five of us will at some time suffer some form of mental illness. Because this study—conducted by psychologists B.P. and B.S. Dohrenwald—looked at a larger number of studies, we will use it and the *Diagnostic and Statistical Manual* (DSM III) of the American Psychiatric Association for our primary sources of information on mental illness and gender. As you read this you should be aware that diagnosing mental illness is a lot more messy and subjective than diagnosing physical illness.

We can dismiss the worst of the mental health problems (schizophrenia) right away because there are about equal numbers of men and women who suffer from it. However, schizophrenia does afflict males more seriously, and up to the age of about thirty-five there are about two male schizophrenics for every female. The risk of schizophrenia decreases with age for men and increases for women, yet another indication that Mother Nature is more protective of women during their reproductive years.

Multiple personality is an area in which the DSM III finds females diagnosed three to nine times more often than males. Despite what many laypeople believe, multiple personality is not schizophrenia. It is a neurotic disorder in which an individual alternates between two or more unique personalities. Dr. Jekyll and Mr. Hyde is a fictional example and "Eve" and "Sybil" are two actual cases that are well known thanks to movies based on their lives. No one has an adequate theory of how multiple personality originates, or why it is more prevalent in women. Some psychiatrists feel that more conformist females subconsciously produce these personalities in an effort to please their therapists. Others feel that it is a form of self-hypnosis related to hormonal swings. Whatever it is, there's many a man who will swear that his wife is as different as night and day at various times of the month.

The neuroses, various emotional disorders characterized by anxiety and phobias, afflict women more than men. Simple phobias like fear of snakes, insects, and mice are about five times more common in women, and more complex ones like agoraphobia (fear of being in public places or situations from which escape might be difficult or embarrassing) are diagnosed about three times more often in women. In the Dohrenwalds' review, all studies showed that the rate of the neuroses was higher in females. Women are also twice as likely to suffer from hypochondria, a preoccupation with pain and illness that has no apparent physical basis.

These differences might not be totally objective. We know that women are more likely to report symptoms, and what man could possibly bring himself to scream in fear of a mouse? But it is true that women have a greater sensitivity and react more emotionally to a wider range of stimulation than men, probably due to the greater sensitivity of their RAS.

Where men really predominate in terms of mental illness is in the so-called personality disorders. These constitute a number of long-standing defects of personality such as alcohol and drug addiction, sexual deviations, and psychopathic personality. Some psychiatrists would not characterize the personality disorders as "mental" problems, but rather as "character" disorders. Many such disorders are kind of on the line separating the mad from the bad. We discuss the personality disorders at various other places in this book.

Marriage is good for your mental health as well as your physical health. A study of New Yorkers found that 25 percent of married men and 19 percent of married women were in "excellent" mental health versus 4 percent and 7 percent of divorced men and women, respectively. When it came to the other end of the scale, those people defined as "seriously impaired," 40 percent of divorced men and 42 percent of divorced women fit the description as opposed to only 19 percent of married men and 20 percent of married women. Other studies show that women are more depressed than men over all marital status categories, and that divorce has a more depressing effect on them. Combined with the data on marriage and physical health, it is pretty clear that marriage is good for most of us most of the time. So go ahead, hug your better half, it'll be good for you both.

LOVE, SEX, AND SELF-ESTEEM

Self-esteem—how well or poorly you think of yourself—is an important part of mental health. Most studies of self-esteem and self-confidence find that men have more of it than women. More self-esteem and confidence usually means greater ambition and achievement. Men's rightward-leaning brains and anabolic hormones drive them to seek action and dominance. It has been said that while men see women as sex symbols, women see men as success symbols. As such, men feel that they have to prove their manhood by achieving; a woman's womanhood needs no proof. Even when men and women achieve equally, men tend to take all the credit for it themselves while women tend more to credit circumstances and luck. The opposite is true in cases of failure, with most men explaining it by bad luck and most women putting it down to their own incapability.

A look at how the majority of men and women gamble in Las Vegas, or what they do at the county fair will show that men are more prone to be engaging in activities in which their skill and confidence can influence the outcome, women are more likely to be playing games of chance. Men play blackjack and show off their killer instincts by knocking over tin ducks with popguns; women feed the slot machines and play bingo.

Intrigued by observations such as this, one psychologist offered men and women an opportunity to play games requiring skill or games involving only chance. She found that 75 percent of the men and only 35 percent of the women chose games that required skill. Pollsters have known for a long time that women are about twice as likely as men to use the "don't know" or "unsure" options in surveys, indicating that women lack a certain confidence in their opinions (or perhaps merely that they are less quick to make final judgments).

Of course, self-esteem fluctuates from person to person and from situation to situation. Male self-esteem tends to flow from their success or failure in the activities they pursue, women's from their success or failure in interpersonal relationships. Two recent studies illustrate this. Each study asked a number of men and women to complete identical self-esteem scales. One study assessed the amount of love male and female subjects perceived themselves to be getting from their circle of friends, relatives, and acquaintances, the other asked about the number of sexual partners they had experienced.

The first study divided the sample by sex and love level as shown in Figure 4. Females had the lowest and the highest level of self-esteem depending on their "love level." They felt great about themselves if they saw themselves as well-loved, and felt horrible about themselves if not. In the second study it was the men's turn to be both top and bottom. Males had both the lowest and highest self-esteem scores depending on their sexual experience, with male virgins having the lowest score and sexually experienced males having the highest score. The self-esteem gap between "low" and "high" love women is particularly striking. Both studies illustrate that "getting it" means two different things for men and women.

Figure 4. Love, Sexual Experience, and Self-Esteem

Love Level	Average Self-Esteem Score	Sexual Experience	Average Self-Esteem Score
Female/low love	31.4	Male Virgins	36.3
Female/medium love	36.4	Female Nonvirgins	38.8
Male/low love	37.7	Female Virgins	39.0
Male/high love	37.9	Male Nonvirgins	41.5
Male/medium love	42.3		
Female/high love	42.9		
High/low difference =	11.5	High/low difference =	5.2

4

Health and Illness

IF YOU'RE SO STRONG, WHY ARE YOU SO DEAD?

There is broad agreement among men that the fair sex is also the weaker sex. Except in the case of sheer physical strength, this belief is pure male schmuck. It is a fact that women tolerate pain less well than men, that they are better able to recognize symptoms of illness in themselves (and admit it), and more likely to visit the doctor (women make an average of 5.5 yearly visits to the doctor, men average 4.0 visits). It is also true that the radical chemical changes in her body during pregnancy, and to a lesser extent during the menstrual cycle, may make a woman prone to sickness more often. But these frequent bodily adaptations may also fortify women and make it easier for them to shake off illnesses that tend to get a firmer grip on men. Women may get sick, but men get buried.

If you don't already believe it, the partial list of illnesses that afflict men at least twice as often as women (or women twice as often as men) presented in Figure 5 should convince you of the constitutional superiority of women.

TOO MUCH Y, YOU DIE

A simple enumeration of differences in susceptibility to a variety of illnesses is not the whole story. Sure, women have to put up with more constipation (and the hemorrhoids that result), headaches (about ten times as often), bladder infections (about five times) varicose veins (about three times) and assorted "female problems," but the ten most deadly diseases, such as cancer,

Figure 5. The Sick List

Illnesses that Afflict Men at least Twice as Often	Illnesses that Afflict Women at Least Twice as Often
Acoustic trauma	Anemia (exclusively)
Acute pancreatitis	Arthritis deformens
AIDS (although women more prone)	Cancer (breast, reproductive tract)
Amebic dysentry	Chorea
Alcoholism	Chronic mitral endocarditis
Arteriosclerosis	Cleft palate
Bright's disease	Gall stones
Cancer (oral, pancreatic, respiratory tract, skin)	Goiter exophthalmic
Cerebral hemorrhage	Hemorrhoids
Childhood schizophrenia	Hyperthyroidism
Cirrhosis of liver	Influenza
Duodenal ulcers	Lupus
Dupuytren's disease	Migraine headaches
Gastric ulcers	Multiple sclerosis
Gout	Myxedema
Heart and coronary arterial diseases (angina pectoris, coronary sclerosis, myocardial infarction, etc.)	Obesity
	Osteomalacia
Hemophilia (exclusively)	Purpura haemorrhagica
Hernia	Rheumatic fever
Hodgkin's disease	Rheumatoid arthritis
Leukemia	Scleroderma
Muscular dystrophy	Varicose veins
Paralysis agitans	Whooping cough
Pigmentary cirrhosis	
Pineal tumors	
Pleurisy	
Pneumonia	
Pyloric stenosis	
Sciatica	
Scurvy	
Sexually transmitted diseases (although women more prone)	
Tabes	
Thromboangiitis obliterans	
Tuberculosis	

strokes, heart attacks, pneumonia, and cirrhosis of the liver attack men at least twice as often as women.

It gets worse. If we take the various organ systems of the human body—circulatory, respiratory, nervous, kidney and excretory, alimentary, skin, skeletal/muscular, and endocrinal—the crackup of all but the immune system is more likely to lead to death for males than for females. Men succumb sooner to fifty-seven of the sixty-four leading causes of death. Women "go with the flow," but men just go.

Despite the greater intestinal fortitude of females, most people, both men and women, feel that life is more difficult for them. A survey of 505 men and women found that that only 30 percent of the women and 21 percent of the men thought it was easier to be a woman than a man. Fifty-nine percent of the women and 65 percent of the men thought it easier to be a man than a woman. What do you think? Before you answer, consider that on a typical day men spend a daily average of about seven minutes on child care while women spend four times as much, twenty-eight minutes, much more when children are preschoolers. Also, men spend an average of fifteen minutes preparing meals and twenty-six minutes cleaning house each day; women spend fifty-one minutes and sixty-five minutes on these activities, respectively. All this despite the fact that 78 percent of married women also work outside the home!

JINXED GENES AND RECESSIVE MESSES

The reasons behind these sex differences in disease susceptibility are a complex mixture of environmental, genetic, and hormonal factors. Men are more active and adventurous, and are therefore more likely to sustain injuries. They are more likely to smoke, drink to excess, work with dangerous substances, and suffer job-related stress than women. But even when men and women have identical lifestyles, women still enjoy a considerable advantage in the mortality tables. Because of this, and because the males of just about all animal species suffer higher death rates than females, we have to look beyond environmental causes for these differences.

The blueprints for making us what we are and for how we function are contained in our genes, which are located on our chromosomes. Chromosomes from dad's sperm are matched with virtually identical ones from mom's egg. Each gene occupies a particular and identical place on both chromosomes, so each gene coding for a trait is represented twice. These paired genes for the same trait are called *alleles,* and they can affect the trait (say eye color) in different ways. If you have genes for blue eyes and mate with another blue-eyed person, all your offspring will have blue eyes. The fact that you and your mate have blue eyes is proof positive that neither of you carry the gene for brown eyes. If you did you wouldn't have blue eyes in the first place because the brown-eyed gene is dominant—it always wins out. If your blue-eyed wife has a brown-eyed child, you should reassess your relationship.

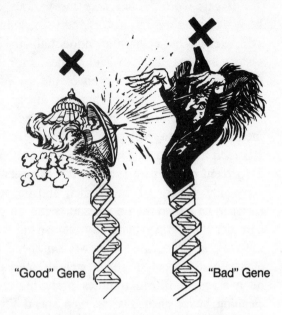

"Good" Gene   "Bad" Gene

Having brown eyes doesn't necessarily mean that you are not carrying the blue-eyed gene. If you are, and if you mate with another brown-eyed person also carrying the blue-eyed gene, there is about a 25 percent chance that you may produce a blue-eyed child. Most often, however, your children will have brown eyes because the gene for brown eyes is dominant over the gene for blue eyes.

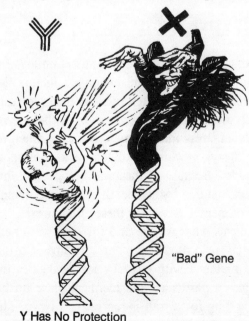

"Bad" Gene

Y Has No Protection

Such genes are called "recessive," and they don't always produce something as neat as a beautiful blue-eyed child. Sometimes the expression of recessive genes represents a mistake in the blueprint that can lead to genetic diseases known as "X-linked" diseases. (Occasionally a genetic abnormality leading to the expression of recessive traits can be advantageous.) As their name implies, the mistake is on the X chromosome. But how does it come about? We have seen that genes and the chromosomes that carry them operate in pairs, but, as far as the sex chromosomes go, the pairing only occurs in females. If you are a female and you receive an X chromosome with a recessive glitch, you have a backup dominant gene on your other X chromosome. So although you carry a recessive gene that you may pass on to your sons, you yourself are protected against any X-linked snafu because you have a double dose of X.

If you are a male, you don't receive a pair of genes for traits carried by the X chromosome because you only got one of them. If that one X has a genetic defect on it, you lack the protection provided by the pairing of a second X. The recessive gene will be able to express itself in the absence of a dominant and vigilant twin gene. The Y chromosome offers no protection from his sister X's foul-up, and can only stand by in horror as she messes up his host's body in some way. Hemophilia and muscular dystrophy are two particularly nasty genetic blueprint mistakes that almost exclusively affect males. For a female to suffer from an X-linked disease she would have to be the daughter of a male sufferer and a female carrier, an extremely rare occurrence.

PAY ATTENTION, YOU LITTLE RASCAL!

We saw in the chapter on the brain that women possess reticular activating systems (RAS) that make them sensitive to some aspects of the environment that a man's RAS may ignore. The female tendency to exaggerate the meaningfulness of incoming information protects her from accidents and illness in a number of ways. Her greater sensitivity to pain makes her visit the doctor at a lower threshold of concern than the typical man might, which can nip many diseases in the bud. Her greater fear of novel and threatening situations will lead her to avoid them more often than many men will, thus lessening her chances of being harmed. Men's need for higher levels of stimulation to be "turned on" (activate the RAS), make them more prone to take risks and to seek high levels of sensation such as drinking, smoking, taking drugs, driving fast, getting into fights, and sky diving. All of this leads to a greater probability of illness and to higher rates of injury, accidents, sickness, and death among men than among women.

RAS alertness during critical periods of infant development is particularly important. Because the RAS controls and monitors breathing and heart rate, it is vital that it be alert to dangers such as sputum accumulation and bed clothing that may inhibit breathing. If it is not, a very young infant may succumb to sudden infant death syndrome (SIDS) or crib death. SIDS is a tragedy in which victims experience respiratory failure during sleep. It is an affliction that is often secondary to RAS sluggishness. Due to the lower level of male RAS arousal, SIDS is at least twice as common among male infants as among female infants.

A sluggish RAS is also related to hyperactivity, which is found to be about five to eight times more prevalent in males than in females. Hyperactive "perpetual motion machines" get themselves into a lot of trouble, and are often unpopular with teachers and schoolmates. Their activity reflects strong RAS reduction and habituation to stimulation, which makes them easily bored with a level of stimulation most of us find acceptable. Although stimulant drugs such as amphetamines make folks with RASs operating in the normal range more active, treatment with stimulant drugs (Ritalin) makes hyperactive kids less active by making the RAS more alert and sensitive to existing stimulation, thus making their frenetic search for hyperstimulation unnecessary.

THE GRASS IS GREENER ON BOTH SIDES OF THE BRAIN

Another female protection is her less specialized brain. We have seen how the two interacting hemispheres of the brain are better integrated in the female, which gives her additional protection against various disorders of the brain just as her extra X chromosome gives her extra protection against disorders of the body. Many types of brain/behavioral disorders—aphasia, dyslexia, autism, childhood schizophenia, psychopathy, for example—that are suffered primarily by males can be traced to the stubborn specialization of the male brain and its relative inability to transfer functions that are messed up on one hemisphere to the other hemisphere.

We can easily see the advantages of having a brain with greater ability to transfer functions from one side to the other. For instance, female stroke victims regain much more of their former functioning than male victims precisely because of the ability of their brains to transfer functions controlled by the damaged side to the undamaged side. Thanks to relatively low androgen levels, Turner's syndrome females (those "exaggerated" females) have even more scattered visual and speech centers across the left and right hemispheres of their brains than do XX females and are thus even more protected from brain developmental disorders than their genetically normal sisters.

HOW LONG TO "SO LONG"?

Life expectancy varies greatly from country to country, and depends to a great extent on a country's health standards. But in no country does the average man outlive the average woman, and although life expectancy increases for both sexes with improved health standards, the gap between male and female life expectancy widens as health standards get better; improved health standards benefit females more than males. In the modern industrialized world there are three women for every two men past the age of sixty-five, two women for every one man at eighty, and four women for every man by the time the hundred-year mark is reached.

The differences in life expectancy *between* different countries point to the impact of environment on life expectancy; the difference between the sexes within each country strongly supports a biological impact. Any suggestion that different work environments and life styles mainly account for male/female differences was largely put to rest by a study of forty thousand white American nuns and monks. All these saintly men and women were free of the stresses of marriage and work (they may not get on with the bishop, but they have job security), none smoked or drank, and all were engaged in teaching. In spite of their almost identical life-styles, the seven-year gap in American life expectancy remained intact.

CUT-UPS LIVE LONGER

If you are a man, one way to increase your lifespan—although we don't think you'll want to take advantage of it—is castration. A study of 297 castrated, institutionalized, mentally retarded men found that they outlived a matched group of noncastrated male inmates by an average of fourteen years. The men had been castrated in the first few decades of this century in Kansas to keep them docile. Removing the testes removed the source of testosterone, making men less aggressive, and less susceptible to testosterone-related diseases. These *gentle*men even lived an average of seven years longer than the average female.

WANT TO LIVE LONGER? GET A SPOUSE

Spouses are good for you? Why, sure; just think of all the things that could happen to a man without a wife—his bank account would get much too big, single women would be chasing him all the time, and he'd sleep late on his days off. A poor husbandless woman would have far too much time for herself, she could go to bed when she wanted to, and she'd never fall into the toilet bowl. All this aside, study after study indicates that married men report significantly higher levels of well-being than unmarried men, and University of California at San Francisco researchers report that single middle-aged men were about twice as likely to die within any decade than were married men of the same age (No, Percy, marriage is not just another form of castration).

Not only do married people live longer, they have fewer illnesses and recover more quickly from those they do get. Much of the greater longevity among the espoused comes from having a wider circle of social support, the aura of established permanence, and the encouragement husbands and wives give one another to stay involved with the world. Although women benefit healthwise from marriage, men benefit more. Wives nag their husbands into visiting their doctor and about their smoking and inactivity, and they fix them nutritious and regular meals. For their part, husbands provide the intimacy women crave, they give their wives a reason to cook healthy and nutritious meals that they might not otherwise bother preparing, and they provide targets for nagging, from which women everywhere seem to derive salutary benefit.

IS MOTHER NATURE A MAN-HATING BIGOT?

It would be easy to conclude from all this that Mother Nature is a female chauvinist sow. She has provided the female with a backup X chromosome, a more efficient pain system to alert her to danger, less bravado so that she will do something about it, and a better stocked internal medicine kit to help her fight it off. Not only that, Mother Nature has provided women with a more efficiently integrated brain and a RAS that makes them pay greater attention to the dangers of the world. She has done these things not because she is a man-hater, but to ensure the survival of the species. No matter how you slice it, you have to come to the conclusion that females are much more valuable to the species than males. Before you pull the hair from your ears, sir, hear us out.

Assume that some worldwide disaster of unholy proportions had occurred. Further imagine that ten virile young men and one very frightened fertile female somehow survived the disaster untouched. What do you think would be the likelihood of species survival? It wouldn't be very good. Five of the men would probably be killed right off the bat fighting over the woman. But no big deal, because even if the victors sensibly decided to share her, only one of them can impregnate her. Assuming she didn't die in childbirth (or from exhaustion) she would be able to produce only one child per year at best. If she died in a couple of years, after bearing (naturally) two boys, it's bye-bye species.

Now consider the opposite: ten fertile women and one very lucky virile man. He could quickly have them all in the family way. Even if half of the women died in childbirth, and let's say that three of the infants also died, he would still have fathered eight children, half of whom we assume will be female. He could then start over again, and then die (happily) two years later having made a good start in replenishing the earth with his own kind.

Doesn't this latter scenario show that it is the male who is more important? No, it does not. One man or 100 men, it would make no difference to species survival. As long as there is only one woman it doesn't look good. On the other hand, the more women there are, regardless of the number of men, the more likely it will be that the species will survive. Unlike the death of the female in the first scenario, the death of the male in the second scenario would be of relatively little importance to species survival. The male's only *necessary* contribution to species survival is the provision of stud service—a few pelvic thrusts, after which he can be on his way. So you see why the female is so important, and why Mother Nature is so protective of her.

THE ENEMY WITHIN

The one major organ system of the body that's more cruel to women than to men is her immune system. Immune system diseases such as multiple sclerosis, lupus, myasthenia gravis, and rheumatoid arthritis attack women about twice as often as men. Oddly enough, this occurs not because a woman's immune system is less efficient than a male's, but because it is *more* efficient. Because nature is so protective of females of child-bearing age, women have hypersensitive immune systems in comparison to males. The immune system attacks outside agents (bacteria, pollen, viruses, and genetically unrelated human fluids and tissue) that it recognizes as not belonging in the host body. Unfortunately, a woman's overzealous immune system sometimes mistakes parts of her body as foreign material and attacks it, and the more efficient it is the stronger is the attack.

THE HEART OF THE MATTER

Heart disease is the number one killer of both men and women in the United States. But the similarity of the sexes in this connection stops there. Women are protected by estrogen before menopause, and they experience 50 percent fewer heart attacks. Although it is true that estrogen promotes the storage of fat, it also causes a decrease in dangerous fatty substances (LDL) floating around in the blood and makes the blood vessels more pliable. Estrogen takes dietary fat and deposits it in body tissues to produce those characteristically feminine curves—fat on the butt is safer (and looks a lot nicer) than fat in the blood.

Postmenopausal women begin to catch up with male heart attack rates as estrogen secretion diminishes (after the ovaries stop producing estrogen the adrenal glands produce some, but only about one-sixth the amount before menopause). Postmenopausal women are actually at greater risk of death from heart attacks than men of the same age. Within the first few weeks of a heart attack women are two times more likely than men to die. Within a year, about 40 percent of women die compared with about 30 percent of men, and within four years women have about a 20 percent chance of a second one, men a 15 percent chance. Before menopause, a woman recovers faster from heart disease than a man. Women who take estrogen supplements seem to have less heart disease than their age-matched sisters who don't.

The average adult male's blood pressure is 140/88; the average female's is 130/80. At age sixty, male and female blood pressure is almost identical at 156/91 and 158/90, respectively. Borderline hypertension (high blood pressure) is often defined as 145/90. After menopause and the loss of hormonal protection, women surpass men in the rate of hypertension with five hypertensive women to every four hypertensive men.

SEX FOR MEDICINAL PURPOSES

Few things in life raise blood pressure higher than the excitement of sexual activity. Cardiologists usually allow recovering cardiac patients to resume sexual activity a few weeks after release from the hospital, but only with their wives because they don't want their patients to become too excited. They are aware that nine out of ten fatal heart attacks resulting from sexual activity occur among men past forty at the Come and Go Motel while partying with playmates other than their dearly beloveds. There's a limit to the excitement an old guy's ticker can take.

But don't be put off—exercise is a great way to improve your heart's efficiency, and having sex is great exercise. It won't help you to shave those extra seconds off your mile or add pounds to your bench press, but it does have health benefits few of us are aware of. Apart from the sheer pleasure, the sense of well-being, and the release of tension experienced after having sex, there are many other health benefits for both men and women that accompany sexual activity. For men, regular sex helps to keep the prostate gland in good working order. The prostate provides the ejaculatory fluid, and regular ejaculation prevents many of the infections that develop when the prostate becomes congested with fluid. For women, many experts feel that regular sex relieves the tensions of premenstrual syndrome (PMS) and provides relief from lower back pain, but only if she assumes the maligned "missionary" position.

Although testosterone is the common source of sexual energy for both men and women, some researchers believe that different neurotransmitters (the brain's chemical messengers) motivate the male and female sex drive. Serotonin is said to best activate the female drive and norepinepherine the male drive. How can we get more of the stuff? Serotonin production is encouraged by carbohydrates, and norepinepherine by protein, so it's pasta for the ladies and beef for the gentlemen. If you eat too much of either you might want to pay attention to the next section.

FATS AND FIGURES

Women catch up to male rates of fat-induced heart attacks after menopause because, as far as nature is concerned, they are no longer reproductively useful. During her child-bearing years she needed all this fat, stored deeper and heavier than in a man to ensure that any pregnancy was sustained.

It takes from 70,000 to 90,000 calories to take a human fetus from conception to birth. The same estrogen that promotes fat retention also stimulates water retention and hunger, all for the benefit of the child growing within her. The extra water and fat assure the fetus of enough sustenance to remain viable should the mother find herself in conditions of famine.

Because of this need, nature makes sure that women will find it more difficult than men to lose fat, especially in the thigh and buttocks areas. This is primarily because of the different distribution of fat receptors in men and women. Fat cell receptors come in two kinds: alpha and beta. Beta receptors release fat a lot more readily than alpha receptors. In the abdominal area, where men tend to accumulate fat, the fat receptors are mostly beta; this is partly why men can lose weight faster than women.

As you might have guessed, in the thigh and buttocks areas, where women most likely store their excess fat, alpha receptors dominate. Women can take *some* comfort in the knowledge that nature has conspired to prevent them from losing weight as easily as men in the name of species survival. Keep that thought with you as you sweat along with Richard Simmons.

CELLULITE: THE FAT FROM HELL

A byproduct of nature's tenacious hold on female fat is cellulite, the hard-to-budge pudge. Cellulite doesn't exist, say some medicos, but the eight out of ten women who stare in the mirror at their cottage cheese thighs and butts know better. It is true that cellulite is not biologically distinct from plain old fat, but those little bumps and ripples are anything but cute. Only the fair sex gets attacked by these devilish dimples. No matter how overweight a man is, he doesn't have to worry about cellulite.

There are a number of reasons why females get cellulite deposits while men don't. We know that estrogen promotes fat retention, particularly in the storage areas beneath the skin between connective tissue. But this isn't the whole story, because women with far less fat than some men still get cellulite. The major reason is the difference in how the skin attaches to muscles in women and in men. The skin is attached to the muscles in women by relatively thin parallel cords. What happens to the 80 percent of women with cellulite is that the valleys formed by these cords fill in with fat. When the valleys are full, any additional fat deposits bulge out through the skin to produce the orange-peel ripple effect. In addition, women's thin skin makes the effect more pronounced than it would in men if they were prone to the same process.

It's not a thicker skin that protects men from the cellulite syndrome, however. Men store fat in an unbroken smooth layer because the cords making the skin-muscle connections are tightly crisscrossed rather than parallel. This crisscrossing eliminates the formation of valleys into which fat can collect and build up into tiny mountain ranges.

The average man needs at least 1,710 calories a day just to maintain basic body functioning, plus an additional 510 to 2,395 calories, depending on how physically active he is. The average women needs at least 1,350 calories a day, plus another 405 to 1,622 to take care of her physical activity.

To maintain good health a man's waist should measure no more than 95 percent of his hips; a woman's should measure no more than 80 percent of her hips. If a man has thirty-six-inch hips, his waist should be no more than about 34 inches; a woman with the same hip measurement should have a waist no more than twenty-nine inches.

Thirty-nine percent of American women and 27 percent of American men take vitamin supplements.

TO BE OR NOT TO BE

In each of twenty countries surveyed in a 1980 study, more women (a ratio of about three to one) attempted suicide than men—but in every country, men were more successful. Over all countries, men were 2.9 times more likely to actually end it all. In the United States men commit 3.2 suicides for every female suicide. The main reason for this discrepancy between attempts and successes is probably that women tend to use the gas stove and drug overdoses in their attempts to do themselves in while men tend to use more violent means, such as hanging and shooting. Seventy-one percent of male and 36 percent of female suicides in the United States use either shooting or hanging. Female methods are much more likely to be successfully countered by medical intervention than are male methods.

Why do more women attempt suicide? Depression is a major factor in suicide attempts and more than twice as many women as men become seriously depressed. Life seems somewhat rougher for women; they are more prone to mood swings over the monthly cycle, and because they are stimuli-augmenters, depression hits them harder and more often. One major study of attempted suicides found that one-quarter of all women's suicide attempts were committed by women who had histories of being battered by their husbands or boyfriends. Men's suicide attempts are most often preceded by some major failure in their lives.

TAKING THE FIFTH

Men are at least five times more likely to become alcoholics than women. Yet women get drunker faster than men, even if they do typically sip their drinks rather than guzzle them down with lip-smacking gusto as many men do. Of course, we all know this greater susceptibility to alcohol is due to women being smaller than men, having more fat cells that "hang on" to booze, and because they have less body water to dilute it. But this is only part of the answer; doctors have long been puzzled why even women with equal size and drinking experience to men get drunk faster. New research has concluded that women have significantly smaller quantities of an enzyme called alcohol dehydrogenase, which breaks down alcohol

I need more dehydrogenase!!

in the stomach. This means that alcohol remains in its undiluted state longer in a woman than in a man, and that's why she'll always be a "cheap drunk" relative to him.

Women become problem drinkers at a later age than men. This suggests a role played by sex hormones in alcoholism because the sex hormone ratios in men and women become less differentiated as we get older. Women tend to lose control over their drinking and descend into alcoholism faster than men, but, as is the case with other illnesses and difficulties, they also seek treatment faster.

Only one man in ten stays with an alcoholic wife (usually because he's one, too), but nine out of ten women stay with alcoholic men. Very few of these women do so because they're heavy boozers themselves. Many do so because they say their man "needs them," or in the futile belief that "he'll change." It's a funny fact that many women marry a man hoping that he'll change—he doesn't—and that many men marry a women hoping that she won't—she does.

If they take time out from their drinking to have sex, heavy drinking males are about ten times more likely to sire girls than are non-drinking males. This has two possible causes. One is that the heavy drinker's sperm might be adversely affected by alcohol, making any XY fetus less likely to survive than a more robust XX fetus. Another reason (and these two reasons probably act in concert) is that drinking lowers male testosterone levels. Generally speaking, the higher the male's testosterone level the more likely he is to sire boys.

The main effects of female drinking in the reproductive area are infertility and/or a greatly increased chance of damage to the developing fetus.

VENEREAL DISEASE: THE INSIDE STORY

According to the HealthRight Organization, women *can* pick up certain genital diseases from toilet seats, and do so far more frequently than men. Overall, women seek medical help for vaginal infections more than for any other problem. It's not just because a woman sits down on the job more often than a man, either (the average seventy-year-old woman has spent about 10.5 months of her life sitting on the toilet, the average man of the same age about 7 months). She is more often afflicted with genital and venereal diseases because of the the internal nature of her reproductive equipment.

Take the various bacterial and yeast infections we call vaginitis. Lots of women know that recommencing sexual activity after a long lay-off can cause vaginitis, and lots of new brides suffer from the dreaded "honeymoon drip," an affliction that leads them to speculate with dread about the nature of their spouse's premarital sex habits. Actually, honeymoon drip is usually the result of nothing more scary than the rubbing action of her partner's penis. What happens is that the friction of the penis against the soft vaginal wall rubs cells off the wall, allowing the bacteria that normally nest there to penetrate deeper into the vaginal layers where they can grow more readily. Because a man's penis dangles on the outside of his body, and because it is covered by skin just like that on his nose, and not by mucous membrane like that inside his mouth or her vagina, it harbors no bacterial nests. Men are lucky in that they have no such penalty to pay for commencing or recommencing an active sex life.

The structure of the female genitals also makes women much more prone to bladder infections such as cystitis than men. Cystitis is the result of bacteria gaining entrance into the body via the urethra to lodge themselves eventually in the bladder. The bacteria have no particular preference for males or females; it is just that the female urethra offers them a shorter journey from its opening to the bladder. The average female urethra is one and one-half inches long compared to the male's eight inches, so that it takes a shorter time for the bacteria to climb up to the bladder. A man's urine stream usually washes them away long before they have a chance to reach his bladder and begin to multiply. Because a female's bladder is significantly smaller than a male's, she feels the urge to void it more often. But this greater frequency does not make up for a urethra that is about five times shorter than a man's in terms of warding off bacterial attack with a urine flush. Additionally, the proximity of a woman's urethra to favored bacterial nesting spots like the vagina and anus makes life even easier for the bacteria, if more difficult for her.

Sexually transmitted diseases are also more frequently found, and are usually more serious, among sexually active women than among equally active men. Nature exacts a nasty toll on women who behave promiscuously. Women are between five and ten times more susceptible than equally sexually active men to most venereal diseases, although men, because of more promiscuous behavior, have actual rates of venereal diseases about twice those of females.

Because she is so acquainted with the various vaginal infections, a woman is more likely to ignore the appearance of any sexually transmitted disease than is a man. National statistics show that about 80 percent of women and 12 percent of men who catch gonorrhea either have no early symptoms or mistake them for something else. The figures for syphilis are a whopping 90 percent for females and 50 percent for males.

Why this discrepancy? If, for instance, the disease is chlamydia, the most common of venereal diseases, women often experience no symptoms, but men often have penile discharge and pain. If a man wakes up one day and sees that his penis is dripping yellow stuff, he immediately thinks, "Oh, Oh"! and runs off to the clinic. A woman may consider it to be another one of those pesky vaginal infections that will soon go away. It does. But in the case of gonorrhea bacteria, the cessation of symptoms merely means that they are entering a latent phase. Untreated, the little buggers will be back with a vengeance, and may eventually cause sterility, arthritis, and blindness. If the disease is syphilis, if left untreated it will eventually destroy a woman's nervous and cardiovascular systems.

Even more alarming are the figures on gender and AIDS infection reported at the 1990 AIDS conference in San Francisco. A women who has sex with an AIDS-infected man is twelve times more likely to acquire the virus than a man who has sex with an AIDS-infected woman. The vagina, harboring many minute lesions through which the virus can pass, is again the culprit. The semen deposits of an AIDS-infected man may reside in the vagina for a long period, whereas the less vulnerable male penis may only be in the vagina of an AIDS-infected woman for a couple of minutes. The female risk of getting AIDS relative to that of the hetero-sexual male is even greater than stated, given that about 90 percent of carriers of the HIV virus are men, many of whom are bisexual.

Oral sex is more dangerous for a female with an AIDS-infected partner because of the danger of semen coming in contact the mucous membrane of her mouth or stomach lining. Because female genital secretions are much less copious, the male is not exposed to the same degree of risk for in-fection if he engages in oral sex.

Added to this is the fact that women give oral sex more than they receive it. Kinsey's early figures on the incidence of oral sexual activity in heterosexual relationships indicated that about 45 percent of males re-ceive fellatio, although only 16 percent reported giving cunnilingus. A more recent (1979) study of 3,600 males reported by the Kinsey Institute in-dicated that 52 percent of them received fellatio and 48 percent gave cunnilingus during their first marriage (why they limited the question to first marriages we don't know). For both males and females, the higher the education level the more likely they are to engage in oral sex.

As of 1990, there has been no reported case of a lesbian being infected with the AIDS virus by sexual means. A survey of 2,400 young male and female readers of *Mademoiselle* found that 26 percent of the women, 35 percent of straight men, and 63 percent of gay men had been tested for HIV infection at least once.

A few studies have shown that women with AIDS die significantly more quickly than men and may suffer a wider and somewhat different range of opportunistic diseases. Remember when "safe sex" meant doing it when your parents were away for the day?

Although women are far more at risk for venereal disease, of the 1,110,000 condoms sold every day, women buy only 40 percent. On average, men spend about ten minutes a day shopping, women spend about thirty-eight minutes. Given what we know about the sexually active female's risk of disease, we think it only condom sense she should spend some of the thirty-eight minutes at the condom counter, don't you?

5

Love, Marriage, and Emotions

FRANKIE AND JOHNNY WERE LOVERS— BUT THAT MIGHT CHANGE

It's the Belinskis' third wedding anniversary. Frankie wants to make it memorable and beautiful this year (they've argued the last two), so with a happy heart and great expectations she prepares her culinary *pièce de résistance*. Johnny comes home from work, late, and pooped as usual. He finds the dining room in darkness save for a lone candle in the middle of the table. His first thought is "the #%&* fuse's blown again!" He tries the light switch to test his intuition, and the room comes to light just as Frankie, only a *little* ticked, enters the room with the champagne. Well, the fuse wasn't blown, but Frankie's surprise was.

Johnny realizes that he has forgotten their anniversary and steels himself for another of Frankie's bitch sessions about what an insensitive jerk he is. But Frankie, knowing she can always bring it up later, lets it go. She sits Johnny down, turns off the light, and brings in the broccoli souffle. Thrown together by their passion three years ago, Frankie and Johnny sit down to their meal feeling now like two very alien creatures. Frankie waits in the flickering darkness for intimate conversation and fond remembrances of things past; Johnny complains that he can't see the potatoes. Frankie runs upstairs insulted and infuriated at what she views as a sarcastic put-down of her attempt to put some romantic spark into their dulling marriage. Poor Johnny, who merely made a statement of fact, wonders what's gotten into her again. Frankie can't get it through her head that Johnny does love her—doesn't he wash her car and pick

"CLICK"

up his own socks? Frankie worries why Johnny doesn't tell her he loves her anymore or bring her flowers; to hell with the car!

There's no good guy or bad guy in this story. For every women who blames Johnny's thick skin for the disaster there's a man who'll blame Frankie's thin skin. The story simply illustrates that emotional life is experienced differently by men and women. Johnny is a male "doer." He shows his love by bringing home the bacon and fixing the faucet (don't forget, he washes her car, too). Frankie is a "feeler." She shows her love by creating little romantic scenarios in which she hopes to communicate in deep and intimate ways. Possessing a RAS that augments stimuli, her threshold for emotion is low, Johnny's reducing RAS makes his threshold higher; the same emotion just doesn't mean the same for both of them. When he is aroused, Johnny's emotions, like his passion, are explosive and quickly spent. Frankie's emotions, like her passion, are slower, longer-lived, and much more subjective.

This difference leads men, with patronizing smiles and stiff upper lips, to think of women as creatures of mere emotion. Drop the "mere" and they're quite right, but it's nothing to be smug about. Emotions exist to serve certain functions, and women know how to exercise them. A women sees life in all its fullness in rational and emotional packages of equal measure.

She arrives at many a truth in her social relationships to which a man, laboring only with "mere" reason, often remains oblivious. A woman's role as nurturer, caregiver, and comforter to such helpless creatures as infants and husbands makes it important for her to be sensitive to emotional messages. We know that mothers are biologically much more sensitive to the sights, sounds, smells, and touches of infants and children than fathers are. But mother's sensitivity wouldn't amount to a hill of beans if it weren't accompanied by an inner voice translating those physical messages into emotional ones reading "love me," "hold me," "take care of me." She worries and fusses and weeps because she is in tune with the discomforts and pains of others in her life. To be "emotional" is to have strong feelings, and that's great as long as those feelings are good ones.

Men are uncomfortable with "unmanly" feelings, and do their darndest to suppress them. When men express emotion it's usually in the form of anger and aggression; they're usually quite proud of that, but many men would never, *never,* stoop to crying. Man's evolutionary role as protector and provider made a different set of emotions useful for him. Easily arousable aggression, dominance, and jealousy were very useful emotions in the competition for food and mates; sensitive Marvin Milquetoasts just couldn't make it in that sort of world. In today's world we see the hormonal legacy of our animal past expressed in emotions. "Womanly" emotions are every bit as useful and necessary as they ever were; "manly" emotions, rare occasions excepted, are mostly destructive and must be held in check by social controls. Think of it—most of the world's criminal codes exist to try to pull the plug on emotions that are typically male!

SCATTERBRAINS REVISITED

What evidence, other than our own day-to-day observations, do we have that women are more attuned to emotional life? Taking advantage of the fact that visual images that are restricted to the right eye are transmitted to the left hemisphere of the brain and vice versa, experiments have shown that women have a far greater ability than men to integrate the emotional content of the limbic system with the rational cortex. It turns out that most men only recognize the emotional content of a visual image when perceived with the left eye, which is transmitted to the brain's right hemisphere. Thanks larger to their "scatterbrains," women recognize emotionally charged images regardless of which eye is restricted, and thus regardless of which side of the brain the information was transmitted to. With both eyes open women can correctly identify emotions displayed by pictures of actors portraying various feelings significantly more often than men. They are also significantly better able to identify the emotional content of taped conversations that have been purposely garbled.

Although it is not as simple as a happy side and a sad side, it's beginning to look as though the brain's two hemispheres are specialized for different emotional expression. The right hemisphere is more involved in responding emotionally to environmental input, especially when it comes to negative emotions. In the normal run of events, both brain hemispheres serve a modulating check-and-balance purpose over the emotional tones of the other. When one hemisphere is injured it allows for the emotional bias of the opposite hemisphere to take command, coloring the person's whole mind with the tendencies of that hemisphere. When the left hemisphere is injured it allows the right to assume control and depression is often the result. When the right hemisphere is injured the results are either emotional indifference or euphoria.

You don't have to bash your brain to know which side is dominant. Because the hemispheres control opposite sides of the body, if you are right-handed your left hemisphere is dominant, if left-handed, your right hemisphere is. Although about 90 percent of of males are right-handed, males are more likely to be left-handed than females, so there is more right hemisphere dominance in males. But handedness is not the whole story. As we have seen, men have slightly thicker right hemispheres than women, and sex hormones are responsible. During sexual differentiation of the brain, the organizing androgens cause a slight retardation in the development of the left hemisphere, thus allowing the right hemisphere to assert itself a bit more relative to the left in males than in females. Because the right hemisphere responds more to stimulation evoking negative emotions, especially negative-rejecting emotions such as hate and jealousy, men are more prone to them than women.

All animals, including the human animal, are self-centered. We have to be, that's the way nature made us. But we concern ourselves with the well-being of others also, and it is no surprise that women tend to do it more often. Men are more self-oriented and women are more other-oriented. A recent national poll found that 70 percent of the women questioned said they do something special for charity at holiday times versus 54 percent of the men, and 36 percent of the women said they felt bad about not giving more time, versus 25 percent of the men. On the home front, for every woman who abandons her children twenty men do. Talking of abandonment, 54 percent of the men in one survey said they would end a friendship if they discovered that a friend was homosexual; only 28 percent of the women said they would. As gauged by the fact that women buy 90 percent of all greetings cards sold in the United States, women love to "stay in touch," and that's good for us as well as for Hallmark.

Psychologist Carol Gillian has done some interesting work on how boys and girls react to moral dilemmas. She posed a question to boys and girls around eleven years old regarding a man whose wife was dying. He couldn't afford the medication that would save her life, so he had the choice of stealing it or letting her die. Boys tended to treat the dilemma as a simple cost/benefit "math" problem: the man should steal the drug, "because life is more valuable than property." Girls tended more to look at the big picture in terms of relationships and to be more future oriented. If the man stole the drug he might be caught and sent to jail; "then who would take care of her in the future?" Girls wanted the man to borrow the money, or to think of some other way to get the drug that didn't involve the possibility of breaking his relationship with his wife.

Paul Pearsall, a psychophysiologist, sees the greater tendency of males to be emotionally self-oriented as a function of their greater brain laterality, and the more "whole-brain" tendency of females as making them more "other" and "us" oriented. He thinks the female orientation is "more in tune with a oneness concept underlying the principle of healthy living in our world and for our world." In other words, the male's development of a sense of self entails a process of separating the self from others, of becoming "one's own man," while the female process, remains "encompassing," with a built-in basis for lifelong empathy. That's a very nice compliment from a man of science, isn't it, ladies?

HIM, HER, AND HORMONES

Hormones, the body's unconscious control system, are released by the endocrine glands, which are ductless glands such as the thyroid, pituitary, adrenals, and gonads, scattered throughout the body. The endocrine system functions similarly for both sexes, but on the whole a woman's is more active. Hormones are released by the glands in response to environmental stimulation. The "fight or flight" response in which stress hormones such as adrenaline are released is the most familiar example. Women's hearts beat faster, their pulse rates are quicker, their thyroids more active, and their metabolic processes are more uneven.

A woman's hormones are mostly "happy" hormones, a man's are mostly "mad." We have seen how estradiol increases nurturing behavior, and how testosterone decreases it in both sexes. Her hormones operate more in cyclic fashion; although his fluctuate, they do so more linearly. Progesterone, whose main functions are to prepare a woman for pregnancy and to prevent ovulation, is a happy hormone. When progesterone levels are high she feels good, sweet, and nurturing; when they are low she feels depressed and bitchy. Whether or not they've given birth, women dream more lucidly of pregnancy, motherhood, and nurturing during periods of their hormonal cycles in which progesterone is high. Women taking progesterone-dominant birth control pills (they operate by fooling her body into believing she is pregnant already) report strong feelings of nurturance and affiliation; if withdrawn from them, women report feelings of hostility and irritability.

The hormonal ups and downs of the female cycle are responsible for much change in a woman's emotional experience. Some suffer the extreme mood swings that scientists have called premenstrual tension syndrome (PMS). Over a variety of studies it has been found that about 62 percent of all violent crimes committed by women are committed in an eight-day period called the paramenstruum—four days prior to, and four days into, menstruation. During this period progesterone levels drop to almost zero, estradiol drops to 50 percent of mid-cycle baseline, and testosterone remains relatively high at 82 percent of baseline. With the "happy" female hormones so low and the "mad" male hormones relatively high, some scientists have speculated that women who suffer extreme symptoms of PMS are more "male-like" during the paramenstruum, partly explaining why they're more apt to be aggressive then. Some studies have found that women's visual/spatial skills increase between 50 and 100 percent during this period of low estrogen and high testosterone.

THE PAUSE THAT DEPRESSES
AND THE LOVE THAT PROGRESSES

After menopause, an event some have called "the pause that depresses," men and women become more alike. A woman's lowered levels of progesterone and estrogen help to "toughen" her emotions. A man's lowered levels of testosterone help him to "soften" his. However, the emotional gap still remains, even if considerably closed. Studies have shown that males become significantly more altruistic and empathetic as they age, but they remain less so than females at all ages. Women do not necessarily become less altruistic and empathetic as they age, but they do become more assertive and "me"-centered. It's a strange fact that postmenopausal women have *lower* levels of estradiol and progesterone than men of the same age. This may partially account for why women generally report greater happiness than men until their mid-fifties, after which men tend to report greater happiness.

Along with the hormonal blurring of advancing age comes something of a reversal in motivations for having sex. In a study we conducted of 425 men and women ranging in age from eighteen to fifty-nine, we found significant differences in motivation among men and women for having sex. But as Figure 6 shows, these differences dwindled to almost nothing as men and women got older. Love remains the primary motive for women at all ages, but physical pleasure becomes more and more important; in fact, it was twice as important for the oldest group of women as it was for the youngest. Among the men, physical pleasure is most important until we get to the oldest group, when love becomes the prime mover. Once out of their reproductive ages and the hormonal maximization of sex differences, men and women come to enjoy what the other sex enjoyed earlier in their lives.

Figure 6. Motivations for Having Sex by Gender and Age Group

	Age 18–30		Age 31–45		Age 46–59	
Motive	Women	Men	Women	Men	Women	Men
Love	67%	31%	52%	39%	44%	47%
Physical Pleasure	21%	64%	32%	51%	42%	40%
Other	12%	5%	16%	10%	14%	13%

A CRYING SHAME

In a University of Minnesota study, 55 percent of the men and 94 percent of the women admitted to crying at least once during the previous month. Women cried about five times more often than men, but then, they've probably got more to cry about. Even if she doesn't receive more "objective" emotional input than he does, she is more sensitive to it due to her augmenting RAS. Because the emotional and rational sides of a female's brain are better integrated, she is more prone to dwell on her emotions and then express them in tears.

Let's say that Jack and Jill experience a similar mildly stressful event (the barber/beautician loused up their hair cuts). He is likely to experience an increase in norepinephrine secretion (the "action" hormone) in his right brain hemisphere (the "action" hemisphere) and angrily stomp about the house casting aspersions on his barber's sexual pedigree. She is likely to experience a *decrease* in both norepinephrine and right hemisphere functioning, flop on the couch, and tearfully announce that she will "simply die" if anyone sees her in such a state. Jill's depression will last up to ten times longer than Jack's anger.

Male crying usually occurs at a much higher emotional threshold and is most often described as a welling of tears; female crying is more intense, with sobbing and flowing tears. Both sexes in the Minnesota study (75 percent of the men and 85 percent of the women) reported feeling better after the cry. Women may also feel better after crying because they have learned of the male's vulnerability to feminine tears. Many men feel guilty about making their mates cry and hoist the white flag. Many women have learned that if at first you don't succeed, "cry, cry again."

Crying is more than a simple emotional reaction to stress offering psychological relief. Analysis of tears reveals that they contain byproducts of stress-related chemicals, and the act of crying helps to rid the body of them more quickly. Crying also tends to decrease testosterone levels in both sexes. Thus crying not only helps to prevent stress-related diseases such as ulcers and heart problems, but also reduces the tendency to respond aggressively to stress. So the greater tendency of women to let loose with tears may help to partially explain her greater freedom from these diseases.

YOU, ME, AND PEA

Much of the misunderstanding between the sexes has to do with the different ways men and women experience emotion. Men and women love one another, but they find it devilishly difficult to understand one another. So let's look at the differences in how the sexes experience love. Being head over heels is an uncomfortable position for us human beings. It makes us dizzy, silly, and miserable. But we also seem to enjoy it immensely. We think you'll enjoy it a lot more if you come to understand the different ways in which the opposite sex experiences it.

Which is the more romantic of the two sexes? We'll bet that most of you—man or woman—will say that females are. Actually, the answer depends on whether we're talking about the rapidity or robustness of romance. Men fall in love faster and more often than women. In all surveys of dating and married couples who said they were in love, both men and women are most likely to say that it was the male who first identified his feelings as love. But once the love bug hits the fair sex, they indulge themselves more in its fantasy and euphoria, and it is stronger and usually longer-lasting for them. So in the initial stages of love men are more "emotional," while in its later stages women are.

Men fall in love faster because they are "objectifiers." They are turned on more strongly to the physical qualities of the opposite sex, which are more immediately perceived than "inner" qualities such as personality, kindness, sense of humor, and all those other good things we want in a mate. Given the male's greater desire for instant sex with a variety of partners, it isn't difficult to see how he interprets physical attraction or lust as love. In matters of the heart, he tends to think more with his gonads than with his cortex.

Although not unimpressed by male good looks, women are much more concerned with attributes such as personality, intelligence, and (dare we say it?) his "prospects." As the bearer and rearer of any children that may issue from a relationship, the woman has more to lose if she makes a wrong choice. The things that concern women take more time to evaluate than do physical attributes, so it's no surprise that love comes a little later for the ladies. Once she has made her choice, however, she also transfers the object of her affections from the cool and rational cortex to the seething subtropics of the limbic system.

Another reason for the difference in the speed with which males and females fall in love may be a natural emotion-regulating love potion called phenylethalamine, or PEA for short. Urine samples of men and women in the throes of love show that they have significantly more PEA in their pee than control subjects not caught up in passion. PEA is stimulant (and mildly hallucinogenic) chemical produced naturally by our brains that is chemically similar to the amphetamines. As with all other brain chemicals, any excess PEA left over after it has performed its task is removed, either sucked back up into the synaptic knob from whence it came or removed by certain chemicals called enzymes that destroy the excess. One such chemical is called monoamine oxydase (MAO). Men have on average about 20 percent less MAO than women, meaning that chemicals like PEA are left active in the male brain a while longer.

Because PEA is a stimulant it is easy to see how some folks can become addicted to it. Laboratory animals fed a steady dose of it become depressed when it is withdrawn and go to great lengths to seek it out. So when our lovers say, "I can't get enough of you," they may be just like junkies talking to their needles. In fact, many "love junkies" are successfully treated with MAO inhibitors—drugs that retard the breakdown of PEA. The effects of PEA go a long way to explaining why we become so "lovesick" when separated from our lovers, and why we "light up" so dramatically when we're reunited.

PEA seems to be nature's way of attracting the sexes to one another long enough to reproduce. In the process, nature adds joy to our lives. But if that were all there was to it, every women would fall into any man's willing arms, making every mother just a mother, and marking each weaning with a new pregnancy. There are rational considerations as well as emotional ones in mate selection, although their respective contributions are difficult to untangle.

PROPOSING AND DISPOSING. PART 1: MARRIAGE

"Marriage is an institution, but who wants to live in an institution?" is an old vaudeville standby. Despite negative jokes about marriage, 93 percent of us tie the knot at some time in our lives. Since we have to live in the institution once we've committed ourselves to it, we would like life within it to be kind to us. Among Americans eighteen to twenty-four years of age, 39 percent of the women have said that a happy marriage is their most important goal in life versus 30 percent of the men. This is surprisingly low for both sexes, but we should remember the limited age range of the respondents. A successful career was the most important goal for 32 percent of the men and 27 percent of the women.

So what do men and women want from each other as prospective mates? On a purely physical level, a survey of eleven thousand men and women conducted by *USA Weekend* found that the physically most-in-demand man desired by the average woman should be thirtysomething, average weight, with brown hair, and between 5'10" and 6'1". The most-in-demand woman desired by the average man should be twentysomething, average weight, brown hair, and between 5'5" and 5'9". Since neither of us fit this tall, dark, and average profile, we'll hurry on to other things.

A poll of 505 adult Americans asked members of both sexes what they considered to be essential requirements for a spouse. As you can see in Figure 7, there was a lot of agreement between the sexes, but also some very interesting differences.

Figure 7. Essential Requirements of a Spouse

Essential Requirement	Males Want	Females Want	Difference
Faithfulness	97%	100%	3%
Intelligence	88%	85%	3%
Ambition and industriousness	86%	99%	13%
Physical attractiveness	41%	19%	22%
Possession of masculine/feminine traits	72%	41%	33%
Well-paying job	25%	77%	52%

So we all like our spouses to be faithful, ambitious, hardworking and smart. The real difference between the sexes is that females, much more so than males, feel it essential for their mates to have well-paying jobs, and that males feel it essential for their mates to be beautiful and feminine much more than females feel it essential that their men be handsome and masculine. It's not that these low percentage characteristics are not desirable in a spouse; the poll was asking if they were essential requirements. So, ladies, it appears that success in the marriage market may be best accomplished by applying all the feminine charm at your command to your properly painted, powdered, and plucked girlish faces and figures. To the men the message is simpler and more direct—provide and conquer.

LET'S MAKE A DEAL

There is a definite "shopping list" quality about mate selection, but male and female lists are different. Nowhere is this more obvious than in the lonely-heart personals. One study analyzed eight hundred advertisements to find out what men and women wanted in a prospective mate and what they emphasized about themselves as selling points. Overall, men tended to want physically attractive females who were younger than themselves; females wanted men somewhat older than themselves who were financially secure. Both sexes knew what the other sex wanted because these were also the attributes they emphasized most about themselves. Similar findings were reported from a study of marriage bureaus in several different European countries, and from the International Mate Selection Project, which involved thirty-seven different cultures.

Age preferences are reflected in actual marriages. In the United States, only about 14 percent of husbands are younger than their wives. In such marriages, wives are an average of nine months older than their husbands. In male-older marriages, husbands are an average of thirty months older— twenty-eight months in first marriages, and fifty-four months in second marriages. Less than 5 percent of second marriages are husband-younger. The peak years for marriage for guys today is twenty-six; for gals it's twenty-four.

Female attractiveness and male solvency are the coin of the marriage market, an observation that led one social scientist to formulate what he called the "ass and assets" theory of love. Unfortunately, while some of us enter the market flush with assets, others enter it with little more than pocket change. We can realistically only hope to make the best bargain that our assets (or your ass) will buy. Like shopping for a car, looking for a spouse boils down to "let's make a deal." A guy with few assets, or a gal who is short-changed in the looks department, is not too likely to be able to pick and choose.

HE'S RICH? I'LL TAKE HIM!

When social class lines are crossed in marriage, females are more likely to marry "up," and males are more likely to marry "down." But if he's rich, honey, you'd better be beautiful. As a natural attribute, beauty is probably evenly distributed across socioeconomic classes. Financially successful men can raid the "lower" classes for attractive females, where they will find willing partners. On the other hand, the financial security that women want is, by definition, concentrated in the higher classes, so "lower class" males are not very likely to find romance among women from classes higher than their own. Not only are "lower class" males unlikely to marry up, they also have to contend with more successful males raiding women from their own class. Overall, women are five times more likely than men to marry into a higher social class. This phenomenon is why census data consistently find that those least likely to marry are women at the top of the social class ladder and men on the lower rungs.

ACADEMIC HEARTACHE

Let's take for an example the marriage prospects for the top and bottom men and women in the academic world. The Carnegie Commission Faculty Survey of 326,306 faculty members found that while marriage prospects increased with an increase in the prestige of the degree held by men, as shown in Figure 8, for women it *declined* with an increase in the prestige of the degree.

**Figure 8. Percentage of Male and Female Faculty
Never Married by Highest Degree**

	Bachelors	Masters	Doctorate
Females	32.6	41.6	46.4
Males	15.9	12.6	8.5
Difference	16.7	29.0	37.9

Some of these folks may have remained single by choice, but choice is hardly likely to account for either the large differences between men and women or the fact that the differences increase dramatically as the prestige of the degree increases. Why? Well for one thing, male egos shudder at the thought of marrying someone smarter than than they are, and only another PhD has a shot at that. But the male PhD, being after all a male, wants beauty more than brains in a spouse. The female PhD has spent nine or ten years getting her degree, making her about thirty when she settles into her career. By that time she will find very few eligible males around who are older than she is. Even if there are, she has to contend with the "smarts" factor, and the sad fact that they are probably looking for someone younger than she. Further arguing against a "choice" interpretation are findings that men are more likely to voluntarily remain single than women, at least until around age fifty-five. After that age, women are more likely to remain unattached, voluntarily or otherwise.

Since we're talking about brains and bodies, a study of 1,017 married couples found that the more education a wife had the thinner she is likely to be, but the more education a husband had the fatter he tended to be. Women who married men with less education than they had were significantly heavier than women who married men with higher education than themselves (you'll be able to figure out the whys of that one for

A man who wears an ear ring will
be a good husband; " He has
bought jewelry and he knows pain! "

yourself by now). The stereotypical "beanpole" husband and "butterball" wife are most likely to occur among couples who are high school dropouts.

A large study of Israeli married couples found that the happiest marriages take place between liberal men and conservative women. This study is supported by a number of American studies that have found the best marriages to be that of nontraditional men and traditional women. The worst possible marriages are between conservative men and liberal women. How come? Well, a liberal or nontraditional man is likely to "allow" his conservative wife more freedom from traditional female roles than she is inclined to want. The opposite matching is obviously courting marital disaster.

PROPOSING AND DISPOSING. PART 2: DIVORCE

When we get married we promise to stay together 'til death; a rather empty promise when you consider that about 50 percent of all marriages will end in divorce. Each day in the United States about 6,500 couples get married and 3,200 get divorced. A hundred years ago there were only five divorces for every hundred marriages. Most divorces occur within the first six years of marriage.

Divorce is even more likely for remarried couples, with a current rate of about 60 percent. You would think divorced people would be more careful about mate selection the second time around, and they probably are. You would also think that they would have learned the dos and don'ts of marriage from the first time around, and they probably did. But second marriages have all the problems of first marriages, plus problems of a different kind. The main problems of second marriages are stepparenting and dealing with ex-spouses. Having stepchildren in the marriage, especially teenagers, doubles the odds of divorce.

What causes divorce? The main cause is marriage. Single people never do it but married people do it often, so the greater the marriage rate the greater the divorce rate. Social factors have a lot more to do with it than biology; people feel less bound by their promises and oaths today than they did in former times, divorce laws are easier, and women are financially more independent. When society removes the barriers to divorce, more people will untie the knot. Nowhere was this more dramatically illustrated than in Stalinist Russia. It was no big deal to slaughter a few million capitalist-minded peasants, but the commissars were moved to tears over the plight of Soviet women. Women, they reasoned, would never be the equal of men while they were obliged to be mothers and husbands (where have you heard that one before?). With all the wisdom we have come to associate with them, the Kremlin cretins passed a bunch of laws to change things, including quick and easy divorceski. Ivans abandoned their Natashas from Riga to Vladivostok, and fatherless kids picked pockets in Gorski Square. The weakening effect on the Russian family eventually alarmed the stubborn Soviet leadership, and the new policies were reversed in 1937. In 1936, the last year of the liberal policy, there were 16,182 divorces in Moscow; in 1937 there were 8,961, and in 1938 there were 5,433.

WHAT DO I DO WHEN MY PEA RUNS OUT?

When social convention allows, more couples will divorce. So what happens to that wonderful love we thought would last forever? As a drug, PEA attracts men and women to one another, but as with all drugs, we develop a tolerance for it. Tolerance is the physical process of the body adjusting itself to a constant drug dosage. If a junkie is to get the same high from a drug used for some time, he or she has to increase the dosage. If the drug is secreted in the brain in reaction to our lovers, there is no way that the PEA factory can produce more from the same person— only a new lover will stimulate the factory to its former production levels. So-called sex addicts are folks who love the PEA, not the person.

Part of the problem with the marriage mart is that we tend to sell (and buy) the sizzle rather than the steak. If we are simply and exclusively attracted to his assets and her ass there is very little substance left when the sizzle's gone. "True" love grows over time through the kindness, respect, caring, and devotion we bestow upon our partners. Love is attachment as well as attraction, and many people value attachment more than attraction. Such people tend to stay together and in love, but such love is more mature companionship rather than the mad gonadal helter-skelter that may once have been felt.

Men may well be ready to move on to another mate after they develop tolerance for PEA, especially if the marriage was based purely on gonadal attraction. Because men are more prone than women to think of love in physical terms, they are more likely to find fidelity difficult when their PEA no longer turns them on. In a recent survey, 45 percent of husbands said that they found fidelity to be "difficult," as opposed to 21 percent of wives; in another survey, 74 percent of females and 77 percent of males answered the question, "How difficult is it to have a good marriage today" with either "difficult" or "very difficult."

The Census Bureau estimates that about 2.3 million Americans are living together without benefit of clergy. Twenty-six percent of the women and 19 percent of the men eventually wind up married to their live-in lovers. Contrary to popular belief, couples who live together before marriage are about a third *more* likely to get divorced than couples who don't. A Columbia University study found that men were twice as likely as women to get antsy and break up the live-in relationship. People who live together before marriage are by nature probably less prone to making commitments—why else would they "just want to try it first"?

The younger the couple are when they marry, the more likely they are to divorce. "Shotgun" marriages (about 15 percent of all marriages) are particularly vulnerable and likely to end quickly, with only about one-third of them still intact after ten years. You are also about 50 percent more likely to get divorced if your parents did than if they didn't.

More women (43 percent) than men (31 percent) feel that divorce is preferable to remaining in an unhappy marriage, even if children are involved. Women file about two-thirds of all divorce petitions. This is probably because at least two-thirds of the time women were the offended party. Check out the divorce column in your local newspaper; the one listed first is always the party who filed.

The odd thing about this is that women seem to suffer more emotionally from divorce and take longer to get over it. Additionally, one study found that women suffer an average 73 percent reduction in their standard of living, while men experience an average *increase* of 42 percent (only about 12 percent of divorced women collect alimony today).

According to University of Pennsylvania researchers, parents of sons are significantly less likely to get divorced than parents who have only daughters. The reason they offer is that fathers of sons are more involved in their upbringing and more concerned about providing them with a good role model.

Eighty-eight percent of divorced women and 77 percent of divorced men say they are happy. If they're so happy, why is it that 78 percent of divorced women and 83 percent of divorced men marry again?

" 'TIL DEATH DO US PART": HAVING A GOOD MARRIAGE

We are not marriage experts, but we have read a lot of research. From all that reading we've come up with our "Ten Commandments" for a happy marriage. We realize that these things are more easily said than done, and that any combination of two people is a chemical mixture of personalities that may blend or explode. But we do believe that your marriage will prosper and thrive to the extent that you can put these research findings into practice while appreciating the difficulties inherent in the cohabitation of two such different creatures as man and woman.

1. The male should be liberal (nontraditional) and the female conservative (traditional) in male/female matters.

2. Do not have unrealistic expectations of "happiness ever after," but do establish the expectation of permanence.

3. Make your spouse your best friend.

4. You should like as well as love your spouse.

5. You should be committed wholeheartedly to your spouse and to the sanctity of the institution of marriage.

6. You should learn to *communicate* openly and honestly with one another. Active listening is an art that men in particular must strive to learn.

7. Show warmth, affection, and appreciation by word and deed often.

8. Both of you should try to give more than you receive.

9. Cultivate similarities of values and attitudes; respect and understand differences.

10. Come to appreciate that *no one* in your life is more important to you than your spouse.

6

What Mom and Dad
Never Told You about Sex

This chapter is X-rated, which is probably why you're reading it first. Nothing quite grabs our attention like sex, but we are surprisingly ignorant about it, especially when it comes to male/female differences in sexual attitudes, perceptions, and behavior. We are not exaggerating the depth of sexual ignorance. A 1989 test of sexual knowledge among 2,000 Americans conducted jointly by the Roper and Kinsey Sex Research institutes found that only 1 percent scored enough correct answers to earn them an A grade. Two percent earned Bs, 14 percent Cs, 27 percent Ds, and fully 55 percent received a failing grade. This really shows that men and women harbor an awful lot of myths and misconceptions about the opposite sex and even about their own. These myths and misconceptions give rise to a lot of pain and anxiety. Let's get right down to the most basic and most visible areas of concern, the genitals.

THE GENITALS

Both men and women worry about their genitals, but their worries are of two different kinds. According to the Hite report on female sexuality, women worry about how their genitals look, and whether or not they "smell down there." Men worry about (what else?) the size of their penis. Perhaps her sharper smell receptors and his better visual-spatial skills have something to do with this.

In a survey of 460 men and women conducted by us, the majority of both men and women expressed satisfaction with their genitals, but women were just under twice as likely (32.1 percent) to express dissatisfaction with their genitals than were men with theirs (17.2 percent).

Never mind what he thinks of his penis, what does *she* think? One survey of 1,500 women asked the question: "Are you satisfied with the size of your partner's penis?" Eighty-eight percent said that they were; the 12 percent who were not satisfied were about equally divided among women who wished their mate's penis were larger and those who wished it were smaller. We have found no poll assessing men's satisfaction with the aroma of their mate's privates (how would one phrase such a question?) but we did find one in which 81 percent of the men were satisfied with the size of their mate's breasts.

Men worry needlessly about the size of their penis because the long and short of it is that the penis is one of the few areas in which all men are indeed created fairly equally. The most ambitious study of penis size conducted so far (actually measured rather than self-reported) was in 1979 by researchers at the Kinsey Institute for Sex Research. Among a sample of 7,042 males of all racial and ethnic backgrounds, the average erect

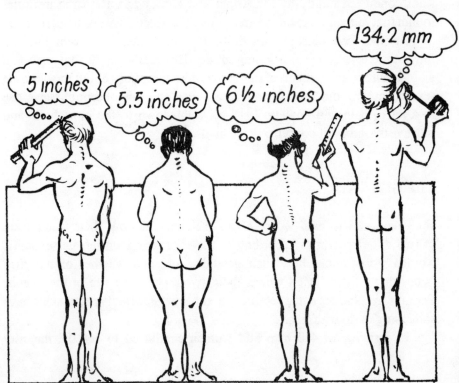

penis was found to be 6.2 inches long (6.15 for whites and 6.44 for blacks). Just over 80 percent of these men had an erect penis length of between 5 and 6.5 inches. The longest penis for which we have reliable evidence was measured at 12 inches, the shortest was one-half inch (this person was an hermaphrodite).

Because of the deeply personal and intrusive nature of its studies, the researchers at the Kinsey Institute rely on volunteers for their information. Volunteers may not be typical of the general population, and it would appear that such people are more interested in sex than the average person. This is something to keep in mind when mulling over Kinsey data. Because penis size is such a sensitive issue for many men, these figures may be an overestimation of average penis size in the general population. After all, men who consider themselves shortchanged in this area would be less likely to volunteer ("Hey, Doc—you won't forget to add my four inches to that total, will you?").

IT AIN'T THE SIZE, IT'S THE MOTION

Researchers stress that there is no relationship between penis size and ability to satisfy your partner (the inner two-thirds of the vagina is relatively insensitive anyway). Nor is there any relationship between body size and penis size as there is, say, between body size and foot size. The largest penis was found dangling on a skinny, 5'7" clerk. Anthropologist Desmond Morris points out that it is a perverse fact that the largest penises are rather consistently found attached to the smallest and skinniest males. Could be Morris is wrong? Maybe the thing just looks bigger hanging between two short, skinny legs.

Although you'd have a hard time convincing them, those few men who do possess an extra long penis may actually be disadvantaged in two ways. First, the bigger the penis the softer the erection. If you've ever seen John Holmes and Long Dong Silver—two particularly oversized porno stars—in action, you'll know what we mean. Their limp equipment performs like a soggy frankfurter being threaded through a stale doughnut hole. Second, during intercourse a long penis can cause great discomfort to a women as it batters her cervix, located four to five inches from the outside of the vagina (now you know why some women who are dissatisfied with the size of their mate's penis would like it to be a bit shorter). This battering may be one reason that cervical cancer is an occupational hazard among prostitutes, and why it is extremely rare among celibate women.

If penis size makes any difference at all, it is the circumference, not the length, that may contribute to greater female satisfaction. During intercourse the thrusting of the penis pulls on the inner lips of the vulva, thereby massaging the clitoris. A thicker penis will accomplish this rubbing more effectively. As Shakespeare put it: "Short and thick'll do the trick." If you're still not convinced, remember that it's the magician who conjures the magic, not the wand. In the above Kinsey study, 78.8 percent of the men had an erect penile circumference of 4.5 inches or less.

By the way, of the 192 different species of primates, the erect human penis is the longest and thickest of all.

Just as a man's concern about the size of his penis is shortsighted, a woman's concern about vaginal odor has the whiff of redundancy. A certain amount of natural vaginal fragrance is designed in by Mother Nature as a sexual attraction mechanism. Scientists call these fragrances pheromones, subtle sexy scents produced by the apocrine glands located under the arms and around the nipples and vulva. These glands are not active until puberty, leading some scientists to claim that the sole purpose of pubic hair is to trap these amorous aromas in the service of love.

Experimental studies show that female pheromones, even when not consciously detected, sexually excite most males. When exposed to female pheromones, men receive an extra surge of testosterone, and even experience a surge in beard growth as a byproduct of increased testosterone.

There is also remarkable consistency among women with regard to the length of the vagina, with about 90 percent possessing a vaginal barrel measuring between 3 and 5 inches long in its aroused state. Just as there is much less variation in erect penis size than there is in flaccid penis size, there is less variation in aroused vaginal size than in unaroused vaginal size.

Here's some food for thought: If the average penis is six inches long and the average vaginal barrel is four inches long, there are about two inches of penis to spare per copulating couple. If we multiply this by the number of sexual active males in the United States, we find that there are about 15,000 miles of unused penis dangling around this country somewhere!

Fifteen percent of a national sample of men thought that the penis was the male body part that most inspired female admiration; only 2 percent of the women agreed. A poll of 322 men and women conducted by us found that women rated the poor penis dead last in terms of male body parts considered most attractive to them. The body parts, in order of appeal, were: face, buttocks, chest, hair, arms, penis. Likewise, the men listed the vagina last, behind face, slimness, breasts, hair, buttocks, and legs. Do you think that these respondents were entirely honest?

According to a survey of men conducted by *Glamour* magazine, a woman's smile is her sexiest asset. A survey of women by London's *Sunday Times* found that the answering Englishwomen considered a man's buttocks to be the seat of his sexual attractiveness. The differences among the various polls in what body parts are considered most attractive obviously depend on what parts are included or excluded.

COMING, READY OR NOT!

So many men risk life and limb in the pursuit of novel sexual thrills that you would think once they found them they would want the encounter to last as long as possible. But unfortunately most men belong to the "stroke 'em and poke 'em" school of copulation. Once they get the go ahead, they're off like Jesse Owens running from a pack of starving pit bulls. According to the early Kinsey reports, the average time from intromission (that means "to put in") to shazzam! was a measly two minutes. Later studies done in the 1980s showed that men have slowed down to a more leisurely average of four minutes. A study of 964 copulating couples by the Kinsey Institute's Paul Gebhard found that only one man in five can last eight minutes or more, and only one in twenty-five can last sixteen minutes or more.

While some may consider two to four minutes quite paltry, it's a marathon in comparison to the promiscuous baboons, who typically achieve climax in a mere fifteen thrusts, which takes them all of eight seconds!

At four minutes a shot, two times a week averaged over a generous fifty-five years of sexual activity, you will have spent sixteen days of your life enjoying intromission. If we assume an average of ten minutes for foreplay (also a generous assumption), you will have spent about five months of your life having sex.

Unless encumbered by the dreaded "brewer's droop," orgasm for the male is a foregone conclusion almost every time he has sex (97 percent of the men in Shere Hite's study of male sexuality said that they always or almost always had orgasm during sex). It's a sadly different story for women, however. Tavris and Sadd's survey of 100,000 American women found that in premarital encounters only 6.7 percent achieved orgasm "all the time," and an astonishing 34.2 percent never experienced it at all. Things improved considerably in their marital sex, with 15 percent reporting that they achieved orgasm "all the time," and only 7 percent reporting that they never did.

The same survey found that women were much more likely to achieve the Big O in a bonded relationship. Only 33 percent of promiscuous women stated that they usually experienced orgasm, but 87 percent of monogamous women indicated that they usually did.

Although men experience orgasm more often, women have more orgasmic *potential.* In the various Kinsey studies it was found that about 14 percent of women are multi-orgasmic (anywhere from two to ten orgasms in one session). Only 2 percent of the men were found to be multi-orgasmic, but "multi" meant two to three orgasms per session (with a fifteen to twenty minute rest in between) for them. The ability to have multiple orgasms increases with age for women and decreases for men.

Despite this greater potential, orgasm is not considered the greatest pleasure experienced during sexual intercourse for most women. In the Tavris and Sadd survey, "feeling of closeness to my partner" was considered the greatest pleasure by 40.3 percent of the women, with only 23.1 percent choosing orgasm. By way of contrast, 83 percent of the 7,000 men in Shere Hite's study of male sexuality said that they could not enjoy sex at all without orgasm.

Ladies, would you rather cuddle or do "it"? A lot of you may remember the famous Ann Landers column in which 72 percent of a very large number of women responded to the same question by saying they'd rather cuddle. Despite the problems involved in phrasing the question as an either/or choice, that's a rather large percentage. No comparable figures are available for men, but you and I know that they would be quite different. According to the Hite study, for men relationships *are* sexual: a kiss here and a tweak there, penetration—whoops! Maybe there's a little cuddling afterwards, but the greater likelihood is that he'll either roll over and go to sleep or jump out of bed to keep his dental appointment. One study did find that 32 percent of males said that cuddling was their favorite thing to do after sex, but 69 percent said it was to go to sleep. Among the women in the survey, 54 percent percent of them said their favorite post-sex activity was to cuddle (42 percent wanted to talk; only 20 percent of the men were interested in replying).

DOING IT YOURSELF

Masturbation is not considered a proper topic of conversation in polite company, but as Woody Allen said, we shouldn't knock it because it's the only time some of us have sex with someone we love. Other advocates of the practice stress that you don't have to look your best or spend a lot of money to get satisfaction. We, however, find it to be a poor, lonely, and impersonal substitute for the real thing.

Fewer women than men admit to masturbating (Kinsey's figures say 62 percent do; Hite's later estimate was 82 percent). A study of two hundred college women in New York found that 33 percent said that masturbation provided them with more intense orgasms than intercourse (46 percent said intercourse did the job better, and 21 percent felt it was about the same either way).

As we all know, women take much longer to reach shazzam than the typical male can last. In fact, statistics from the *Hite Report* found that less than 30 percent of women are able to reach orgasm on a fairly regular basis during intercourse without clitoral stimulation. However, Kinsey's study of two thousand women found that 69 percent could reach orgasm by masturbation in five minutes or less—about the same time as males who take matters into their own hands.

About 95 percent of the men in the Kinsey study admitted frequent masturbation (99 percent in the Hite study), and they do it about three times more often than women. Hite reported that "most" men (she didn't give figures) said that they received more intense orgasms from masturbation than from intercourse, although intercourse was still the preferred way of achieving it.

GETTING THERE IS HALF THE FUN

The initial sensation of orgasm is similar for men and women, and is described as a "sensation of inevitability." But the similarity ends there. While a woman's "sensation of inevitability" can be interrupted at any stage, a man's is almost impossible to stop once the mechanism is in motion. Nature meant the male to have hair-trigger orgasms. After all, nature is interested in reproduction, and the sooner it's accomplished the better from her point of view. Man's orgasm serves the important reproductive function, but woman's orgasm is reproductively irrelevant. All in all, man's

only reproductive function is to ejaculate; woman's is to menstruate, gestate, and lactate. If you didn't know it already, there's a strong urge to discontinue sexual activity once orgasm is achieved. If women reached it with the same speed as men, each sexual encounter would be a fifty-fifty ballgame, and activity might cease before the biologically important event occurred.

The male orgasm lasts about ten seconds; a woman's orgasmic spasms last an average of about fifteen to twenty seconds. If you are a man, and if you average two sexual encounters per week over fifty-five years of activity, you've had 15.9 hours of orgasmic ecstasy; if you are a women who makes it every time, you've had 23.9 hours. Not much is it, for all that trouble?

One large survey reported that 75 percent of the men and 37 percent of the women stated that they "always" enjoyed sex (55 percent of the women and the other 25 percent of the men said that they "usually" enjoyed it). The same poll found that men had sex an average of 2.52 times per week versus 2.97 for females. Are some females having sex alone, or is it just so bad that it just seems to them that they're having it more often?

DO YOU REALLY WANT TO KNOW?

Sex is perfectly natural, but it's not naturally perfect. Zoologists tell us that the human species is the only one in which the female achieves orgasm, making the human male the only one who worries about it. How can a man tell if his woman has had an orgasm? Please don't ask her—women really hate the question: "Did you come?" or "Honey, was it good for you?" If you demand an answer, whether she did or didn't, she's likely to answer in the affirmat've so you won't get your feelings hurt. In Shere Hite's survey of 1,664 females, 53 percent of them admitted that they had faked orgasm on occasion. No man, of course, has ever been with such a woman. According to sexologist Dr. David Reuben, the only accurate sign of a female orgasm is nipple erection—no erection, no orgasm. The so-called "sexual flush"—a rash-like coloring around the ribcage, breasts, and neck—is also a good sign, but some orgasmic women never get it (the flush, that is). Now that men know how to check you out, ladies, it will be more difficult to fake it. But if you think faking orgasm is difficult, imagine what it's like trying to fake an erection.

CHASTE OR CHASED: HOW MUCH IS ENOUGH?

Evolutionary biologists and other scientists assure us that males tend toward promiscuity in sexual relations and that women tend toward monogamy. According to a national sample of adult Americans ranging in age from eighteen to seventy-five conducted by the National Opinion Survey Center, males have had an average of 12.26 sexual partners and females an average of 3.32 since the age of eighteen. Unfortunately, this survey did not break down these figures by sex of partner. According to some estimates there may be many as ten times more gay men as lesbian women (we'll tell you why later), and since we know that gay men get the urge to merge more frequently, the above figures may be a little suspect in terms of heterosexual averages.

According to Glen Wilson in his book *Love and Instinct,* gay men may have as many as a thousand partners over a lifetime, straight men ten, straight women five, and lesbian women only two or three. (The extraordinary monogamous nature of lesbian relationships goes a long way to explain why no sexually transmitted case of AIDS has yet been found among this group). These are typical figures found in samples of many different populations. But we must remember that there is overlap in male/female figures, with some women having a number of sexual partners well in excess of the male average, and some men, believe it or not, having fewer partners than the female average.

Social scientists will tell you that the difference in numbers of sexual partners represents "social learning." "Real men," they will say, are encouraged to be studs, sailing the sexual seas and dropping their anchors in any friendly port. Females are supposed to be "nice girls" and to keep their sails furled until safely espoused. No doubt such social messages are sent, but they are received by men and women who are biologically receptive to them. We, and many other biologically oriented scientists, believe that far from enhancing sexual differences, the process of socialization actually often minimizes them. Think of how differently you behave in groups consisting only of members of your own sex, and then contrast this with how you behave in sexually mixed groups. We have to compromise our inclinations when in the company of the opposite sex. Gays and lesbians do not have to compromise since they mingle sexually in same-sex circles. Isn't it ironic that it is these sexually "deviant" men and women who best conform to the social messages of what "real" men and "nice" girls should be sexually?

Not only do gay men have more partners than straight men and lesbians fewer partners than straight women, in the context of coupled relationships, gay men have more frequent sex and lesbians less frequent sex than straight males and females. In a study of 693 straight, 309 gay, and 357 lesbian couples together two years or less, sociologists Blumstein and Schwartz found that 53 percent of the heterosexual, 67 percent of the gay, and 33 percent of the lesbian couples had sex three or more times per week. For a larger number of couples together from between two and ten years, these percentages dropped to 27 percent, 32 percent, and 7 percent, respectively.

Another Kinsey study reinforces the gay/lesbian differences, as well as male/female differences in general. In their interviews with lesbians and straight women, the Kinsey folks found that only 20 percent of the lesbians and none of the heterosexual women had experienced homosexual oral-genital contact before age nineteen. By way of contrast, 72 percent of the homosexual males and 15 percent of the heterosexual males had experienced homosexual oral-genital contact by age nineteen. Thus almost the same percentage of heterosexual men as lesbian women had experienced homosexual oral sex before age nineteen.

We don't mean to imply that straight men are more "moral" than gay men, or that gay men have stronger sex drives. Straight men would doubtless be as sexually active as gay men if they did not have to compromise with the sexual strategy of females, who are much less disposed to engage in impersonal sex. Gay partners, being both males, do not have to compromise with a different strategy, so they get right down to the business at hand—sex.

You might be saying, "Now wait a minute, how can male and female averages be different? Surely heterosexual male and female averages must be equal. Doesn't each unique partner for a male necessarily mean a unique partner for a female?" If we knew the number of partners every man and women in the country has had, added them up and then divided by the number of men and women in the population, respectively, the figures would have to be identical. But this does not preclude that most females are much less sexually active than *most* males. Extremely active females such as prostitutes and "nymphomaniacs" are not fairly represented in surveys because of their relative rarity (they're too busy doing it to spare the time to fill in questionnaires anyway).

Remember, "average" means that the numbers reported by each person in a survey are added up and the sum divided by the number of people polled. Averages are greatly influenced by extreme cases and don't mean much when the chaste and the monogamous are dumped in the same sex pool with the Wilt Chamberlins, Warren Beattys, and Madonnas of this world. Putting everyone in the same pot is like averaging income among working stiffs with a few billionaires thrown in. (Parenthetically: we hope none of you took Wilt Chamberlin's claim that he has made more broads than baskets seriously. His claim of twenty thousand sexual partners would be difficult to achieve: if he had one new partner each and every day, including Sundays and holidays, it would take 54.8 years to reach that figure. Wilt's a tall man who is obviously a lover of tall tales.)

Better indicators of the "average" in this case are numbers called the mode and the median, which are hardly at all influenced by extreme cases. The mode is the most typical number, and the median is the number smack in the middle of all the observations laid out from the lowest number to the highest. From a variety of studies it has been found that the modal number of sex partners for men is five, for women, three. This means that more men reported five partners and more women reported three partners than reported any other number. The median for men is eight, for women, four, meaning that half the men surveyed have had fewer than eight partners and half more than eight partners. Change the number to four and ditto for women. We're not such a promiscuous lot after all.

About 65 percent of males and 45 percent of females admit that they have slept with someone on the first date. Although men are quite happy to add a first date conquest to the notches on their bedpost, a national sample of 815 American males found that fully 67 percent of them did not like women who gave their favors away too easily, especially on the first date. Men like—and fall in love with—women who are not too anxious to "please" their dates early in the relationship. So ladies, it's true that they don't respect you in the morning. One survey found that 40 percent of the women and 16 percent of the men regretted having premarital sex.

In her book *Psychology of Women,* Judith Bardwick concludes from a variety of studies that most women yielded to their first sexual experience either because of force or out of a sense of obligation rather than their own desire. Women often view sex as the "price" of a romantic relationship, says Bardwick, or a way to prove their love. Her research is a vindication of sorts of the age-old saying: "Men give love to get sex and women give sex to get love."

It's not that women don't like sex; they just prefer it within the confines of a bonded relationship. A poll of over four thousand people conducted by the British daily newspaper *The Sun* found that most women preferred to wait for a commitment before having sex, but few of them actually did—that compromise factor again.

In the same survey, one-third of the men wanted sex at the first possible moment in a relationship ("Hi, my name's Bill. Let's do it!"). Only 9 percent of the women were in a similar hurry. Most men in the survey wanted more sex with more partners and were interested in trying new things. Of the women who wanted more sex, overwhelmingly they wanted more "straight" sex with their present partners. Love and sex are obviously much more integrated themes for women than for men.

Speaking about compromise, a couple of recent studies uncovered the fact that the less attractive females considered themselves to be, the *more* sex partners they had had. Apparently after surveying their assets these women felt that if they were to become involved with a man at all they would have to follow the typical male strategy or be left out in the cold. Women who considered themselves more attractive felt less need to compromise and were able to follow their own natural inclinations. The opposite was found for males: the less attractive they found themselves to be, the fewer sex partners they had.

A poll conducted by *Playboy* shows that the double standard is alive and well in America. But surprise!—females were more likely than males to condone it! When asked if premarital sex was okay for males in situations without strong affection, 60 percent of the males and 37 percent of the females replied that it was. When asked if the same behavior was okay for females, 44 percent of the men said it was, but only 20 percent of the females agreed.

COUNTING VIRGINS

Virginity seems to be going the way of the dodo bird. Among Morton Hunt's survey of married people aged eighteen to twenty-four, 5 percent of the males and 19 percent of the females said that they were virgins on their wedding night (the figures for those fifty-five years of age and older were 16 percent and 69 percent, respectively). So although females don't condone it, they do it.

In a recent *Seventeen* magazine survey, 32 percent of teenage males said that they wanted to marry a virgin; 22 percent of the girls did—good luck!

A large survey of ten thousand people in thirty-seven different cultures called the *International Mate Selection Project* found that while most men found it desirable that their prospective mates be virgins, virginity is losing its status as an *essential* condition. Men in more traditional countries still found it fairly essential, especially in Ireland and in Middle Eastern cultures, but men in most of the Western world today seem not to be particularly concerned with whether their prospective mates have lost their virginity—as long as they've still got the box that it came in.

GAY MATES AND LESBIAN LOVERS

Estimates of the number of homosexuals in the United States range from a low of 1 percent to a high of 10 percent. Differences in estimates may be a function of how liberally homosexuality is defined. The high estimate may be correct if we include those males who from time to time want to experience both ends of the stick (so to speak), and the low estimate may be correct if we confine the definition to those who are and always have been exclusively gay. Homosexuality as an abiding trait is puzzling given the strong evolutionary bias in favor of heterosexuality. But it is now not quite so puzzling why some authorities estimate that there may by as many as ten times more Adam and Steves than Elsie and Eves.

After years of blaming smothering mothers and hostile fathers, science is now coming to the conclusion that homosexuality is in the brain. We saw when discussing the brain that it has long been known that a cluster of neurons in the hypothalamus known as the third interstitial area of the anterior hypothalamus (INAH 3) is twice as large in straight men as it is in straight women. Research has shown that it is also twice as large in straight men as in gay men. No research has yet been done to assess INAH 3 size in lesbians, but it would be interesting.

None of this explains why the surplus of gays over lesbians, but the fact that the male brain represents a diversion from the standard human pattern suggests that homosexuality may be a botched detour on the road to masculinity, with the brains of exclusively gay men retaining more of their original female form. Whatever hormonal accident or accidents may happen, they occur after the male's genitalia are formed; it is the male gonads that release the hormones to modify the brain. In cases of incomplete brain diversion we have partially male-sexed brains in otherwise male bodies. Because the female brain is neither added to nor subtracted from in the normal course of female development, fewer things can go wrong with it (CAH females are more sexually active than hormonally normal females, and there is evidence to suggest that they are more likely to be lesbians).

If gayness is literally "in the head," scientists reason that gay brains should mimic the female response pattern to luteinizing hormone (LH), a hormone that stimulates secretion of estrogen from the ovaries which, in turn, further stimulates LH. American psychoendocrinologist Brian Gladue and his colleagues decided to test this by injecting a number of straight and gay men and straight women with estrogen. The women showed the typical female "positive feedback loop" of estrogen-LH-estrogen (other hormones are also involved). In straight males, the estrogen resulted either in reduced LH levels or no hormonal response at all. LH levels in the gay men showed a secretion pattern midway between those of straight men and women, as if LH were trying to stimulate a phantom ovary. Similar studies with bisexual men find the typical male response to estrogen injections, strongly suggesting that their homosexual behavior is learned rather than physically in the brain.

When we use the words "wrong," "botched," or "blame," we are not making moral statements or engaging in gay bashing. We only mean that the gay brain is a statistical departure from the normal male brain in those parts that regulate sexual preference (but not the sex drive, which is very much in the male direction). The realization that gays are born rather than made means that gays have not made a "wrong" sexual choice any more that straights have made a "right" one. Most gays are delighted with these findings, and certainly anxious parents of gays can stop blaming themselves for their sons' sexual orientations.

NO SEX, PLEASE; I'M TRYING TO LOSE WEIGHT

A man burns calories at the rate of 360 per hour having sex, or about the same rate as playing a round of golf. A woman burns about 240 calories per hour having sex (she would burn them at the same rate doing the ironing). Don't plan on using sex as a weight reducer though—four minutes means you've only used up about twenty-four calories if you are a man, sixteen if you are a women. Both of you probably burned up more undressing, washing off, and getting dressed again.

The number of calories you burn having sex naturally depends on the frequency, intensity, and duration of your activities. Let's say you enjoy intromission for twice the average time and have enthusiastic sex three times a week for a year. Without counting the calories expended during foreplay, a man will use 7,488 calories per year, a woman 4,992. It takes the expenditure of 3,500 calories to lose one pound of weight. All other things being equal, which they never are, a man will be 2.14 pounds lighter after a year, a woman 1.43 pounds lighter. There are numerous more efficient ways to lose weight, but none nearly so nice.

SEXERCISE

Exercise pumps us up and primes us for passion if we can believe a survey of eight thousand women who engaged in regular aerobic exercise. Conducted by *American Health* magazine, the study suggests that exercise functions as a natural aphrodisiac. After beginning their exercise programs, 40 percent of the women said that they were more easily aroused, 25 percent said they were better able to achieve orgasm, and 30 percent reported they had sex more often than they did before. Other studies have shown that the sex lives of men and women in their forties and fifties who exercise regularly are as vigorous—sometimes more so—than men and women in their twenties and thirties who don't excercise.

Some scientists speculate that exercise stimulates testosterone, which stimulates the libido. Others emphasize the chloresterol connection, stating that exercise improves the ratio of HDL (good) to LDL (bad) chloresterol. Over time, this improvement will increase blood flow throughout the body, including blood flow to the penis, thereby improving male erectile ability. Let's hear it for Jane Fonda!

TESTOSTERONE AND THE TIME OF YOUR LIFE

Testosterone is nature's own aphrodisiac, and the only reliable one. Both males and females rely chemically on testosterone for the strength of their sexual desires. Testosterone levels in males peak around the ages of eighteen to twenty-one, and, if you remember, sir, that's when your sexual drive was at its peak. Your testosterone levels steadily decline after that, especially after age fifty. By the time you are around sixty your testosterone level will be about the same as that of a ten-year-old boy.

In females, testosterone levels begin to rise in the mid-thirties; that's when you'll most likely be at your horniest, ma'am. It's a pity that nature couldn't have synchronized these things a little better. Female testosterone peaks during ovulation (the middle of the menstrual cycle). Nature has fixed it so that women are most likely to be responsive to sexual overtures at the times when they are most ripe for fertilization.

Sexual activity peaks according to the calendar are also different for males and females. Sexual activity peaks for males (as does testosterone) in September. Guess when it tapers off for women? You've got it—September! The fact that a disproportionate number of births occur in late spring/early summer (about nine months after the male peak) indicates that sexual activity is geared more to male rather than female sexual peaks.

MAKE PLAY WHILE THE SUN SHINES

Wine, soft music, and a moonlit night: a great scenario for lovemaking, right? Wrong! Quite apart from the negative effects of alcohol on sexual performance, darkness inhibits sperm production and testosterone. Dark-

T-time

ness is an evolutionary signal to slow the body down for rest, telling the pineal gland in the brain to produce a substance called melatonin, a hormone that inhibits the secretion of sex-related hormones. During the daytime, light entering the eyes stimulates neurons that tell the pineal gland to shut off the melatonin so that we are ready for action again. So, while sex under the moonlight is romantic and fun, if you can get away with it you'll probably perform better under the sun.

All this shows us the importance of testosterone in our sex lives. Testosterone is produced in the male testes, so if he is unfortunate enough to lose them it's more or less curtains for his sex life, although in some rare cases the effects are not fully felt for years afterwards (he'll still get a little testosterone from his adrenal glands). A women's testosterone supply is pumped out about fifty-fifty by her adrenal glands and her ovaries. If a women loses her ovaries, which she often does because of hysterectomy, it has no effect on her sex life, suggesting that only adrenal androgens are important in this respect. Only if a woman's adrenal glands malfunction does her libido collapse.

When women receive testosterone for certain medical conditions such as menstrual difficulties, they report a definite rise in their sexual urges.

Males receive no increase in their libido if they are given shots of testosterone unless they are severely short-changed to begin with. Given the high "normal" male level of testosterone, any addition has no effect. Small additional amounts effect women because they have low levels to begin with.

DREAM LOVERS

A woman's dreams are friendly things peopled with more women than men. If she dreams about the opposite sex it's much more likely to be sentimental and romantic than sexual. No need to tell you that it's exactly the opposite for men. Men's sexual dreams tend to begin right at the moment of sexual activity and to be with novel partners. When women have sexual dreams they tend to take some time before cutting to the action (just as they do when awake) and tend to concentrate on the current real-life lover.

In males erotic dreams first occur with the hormonal surges of puberty and are quite frequent. They do not normally occur in females until they are in their twenties or until they've actually had some sexual experience. Even then most women do not have nearly as many erotic dreams as men.

Although we might try to explain this culturally by saying that women are taught that they shouldn't have such dreams, erotic dreams do occur at puberty for late-treated females with congenital adrenal hyperplasia. As we've seen, these women received excessive amounts of male hormones during fetal development, leading to some degree of masculinization of the brain.

One study of erotic dreaming reported a curious sex difference. Among women described as "promiscuous" (women having had ten or more sexual partners), 70 percent reported that they were ashamed of their sexual dreams. Among women who were sexually experienced but not promiscuous, 29 percent were ashamed of them. The opposite was true for males, with 44 percent of the sexually experienced and 27 percent of the promiscuous males reporting that they were ashamed of their sexual dreams.

FROLICS IN FANTASY LAND

Do you fantasize while you're having sex with your partner? In one study 51 percent of the men and 37 percent of the women admitted doing so. Of course, it would be just too lonely not to fantasize while masturbating, but it seems to us that fantasizing about sex while you're having it with a partner you value is rather redundant, like thinking about Dracula while watching *Jaws*.

According to Masters and Johnson, the most frequent fantasy for both men and women during masturbation is about a new or different partner. When asked to describe their fantasies, men report themes of domination and tend to emphasize the minute details of their partner's physical appearance, especially their breasts, buttocks, and genitals, and the sexual acrobatics they perform together. Women emphasize the romantic aspects of the fantasy, with little or no mention of physical appearance or the mechanics of the sex act. If body parts enter into the fantasy they are nonsexual parts such as eyes and hair.

The second most frequent fantasy for both sexes is being raped by a member of the opposite sex. The similarity ends there. Many men, safe in the assumption that it couldn't happen (at least not with a female assailant), say they would fight it with all the power in their pinkies. Women, on the other hand, are overwhelmingly repulsed by the idea of it actually happening. For a woman it's more like a fantasy of being overpowered by a man in a romantic sense and has nothing to do with getting her teeth knocked out by some sweaty, foul-breathed imbecile with a knife. The nice thing about fantasy is that it edits out all the bad parts.

7

Sex and Dirty Business

RAT AND SNAILS AND SUGAR AND SPICE

This chapter is a kind of potpourri mostly addressing the "dark side" of sex differences. The old ditty that told us boys were made of "rats and snails and puppy dogs' tails," and that girls were made of "sugar and spice and everything nice," is a moral metaphor We think that men and women alike have come to regard typical female behavior to be morally superior simply because it is. Can you think of any behavior that is more typically female than male for which it has been deemed necessary to pass prohibiting laws? Neither can we, but we can write long lists of behaviors that are more male-typical for which prohibiting laws exist. You might think of prostitution, but the sex-for-sale merchants, males as well as females, wouldn't exist were it not for their exclusively male clientele.

AFFAIRS MOST FOUL

Although almost all men and women feel that faithfulness is an essential requirement for their spouses, many do not feel duty bound by it themselves. In a national representative sample of 1,401 American adults reported in *Family Planning Perspectives,* 35 percent of the married women and 60 percent of the married men said that they had been unfaithful at some time during their marriage or marriages. It's difficult to get an accurate picture of this kind of behavior, but the figures are fairly consistent with lots of other studies reviewed by psychologist Annette Lawson. She estimates that 65 percent of married men have had at least one affair (72 percent

119

in the Hite report). Tavris and Sadd's survey of 100,000 married women found that 29 percent of them had had an affair sometime during their marriage or marriages.

These figures don't provide us with an accurate picture of the real difference between the sexes in receptiveness to extramarital affairs—adultery, if we are to call a spade a spade. Differences between men and women are magnified when we consider the different *opportunities* for adulterous sex experienced by them. Any woman (well, almost any woman) who is so inclined could easily attract novel sex partners by cooing at the front door in her skimpies; any man doing the same would attract only the police. Most females are discriminating and do not give their favors lightly. A woman who doesn't have adulterous sex usually doesn't because she doesn't *want* to have it, not because of lack of opportunity; a man usually doesn't because he lacks opportunity, not desire. This coupling of female reticence and male desire in what has made rape and prostitution such constant features of human history.

There is a strong association between marital quality and extramarital affairs for women. In the Tavris and Sadd study, 19 percent of the women who rated their marriage "very good" had extramarital sex versus 65 percent who rated it "very poor." The women in "very good" marriages regretted their limited indiscretions while women in "very poor" ones tended not to. Studies do not find this association among men. The male tendency to separate love from sex means that happily married men are almost

as likely as unhappily married men to have affairs. Because a man has adulterous sex just for the sex, he is probably speaking the literal truth when he tells his wife, "She didn't mean anything to me." She has difficulty understanding this because if she were the culprit it would certainly have meant something to her.

In a large West German study it was found that 46 percent of the men and 6 percent of the women "certainly would" or "probably would" engage in sex with an attractive partner other than their steady mate if the opportunity arose. On the other hand, 68 percent of the women and 24 percent of the men responded that they were "rather sure" or "sure" that they would not. Twenty-six percent of the women and 30 percent of the men were "unsure."

Most extramarital affairs involve a little bad sex and a lot of time on the office telephone. They are "fatal attractions" that generate guilt (they should), and they can be very destructive to the marriage and to the individuals involved. We told you earlier that nine out of ten fatal heart attacks suffered by men while having sex occurred when they were having adulterous sex; so next time you get the urge to merge with someone other than your wife, just think how embarrassing that would be.

About half the wives who catch their husbands with their hands in the nookie jar divorce them, but about 80 percent of the husbands who catch their wives *in flagrante delicto* do. This inclines us to believe the many studies showing that men are more possessive and jealous than women. Some authorities believe that jealousy is selected in by evolution to minimize the possibility of cuckoldry (a cuckold is some poor guy who raises and provides for the child of an unfaithful wife and her lover believing it is his own). After all, it's an awful truth that all children are really "mommy's babies and daddy's maybes."

LET'S FINALIZE THIS IN MY OFFICE: SEXUAL HARASSMENT

As the Supreme Court nomination hearings of Clarence Thomas vividly brought home, few things underscore the gender divide more than attitudes about sexual harassment. Although there must have been some overlap between "politically correct" men and "get real" women, about 100 million of us (the men) saw the allegations against Thomas as a storm in a teacup, another 100 million of us (the women) saw them as "Hurricane Clarence." We venture to say that almost everyone of either sex would agree that demanding sexual favors in exchange for employment or promotion is absolutely wrong. The gender lines are drawn more sharply when the issue is sexual banter, innuendo, flirtation, and jokes. While many men tend to see these things as harmless fun, many women are truly offended. From their own sex-based perceptions, both men and women are absolutely right.

One poll introduced as testimony in a Florida harassment case found that while 75 percent of the women polled would be offended by sexual advances in the workplace, 75 percent of the men said they would be flattered. A few men have filed complaints of sexual harassment, but they are usually cases of harassment by a male boss. In one newspaper survey of 650 working men and women, 65 percent of the women said that they had been sexually harassed on the job at least once. Less than 2 percent of the men reported that they had, but many others are patiently waiting.

POLYGAMY: WILL YOU, YOU, AND YOU MARRY ME?

Are humans naturally monogamous or polygamous? Most evolutionary biologists will say that it depends on whether we're talking about men or women. The tendency throughout the mammalian animal kingdom is for female harems to form around a single male, but there is no evidence of the reverse. We also see this pattern in polygamous marriages throughout the human world.

Polygamy is a general term for two different marriage forms—polygyny and polyandry. Out of 849 human cultures listed in the *Ethnographic Atlas,* 709 (83.5 percent) are polygynous (one man, two or more wives), 137 (16.1 percent) are monogamous (one man, one wife), and 4 (under one-half percent) polyandrous (one woman, two or more husbands). Although most *cultures* in the world are polygynous, most *marriages,* even within cultures allowing for other marriage forms, are monogamous.

Polyandry and polygyny are not sexual mirror images. Sexual variety is undoubtedly a motivator (among others) for a man to take extra wives in a polygynous culture, and the choice to take them is his to make. Polyandry is overwhelmingly fraternal—two or more brothers sharing the same wife. Wives in such cultures have little or no say in the matter—if her husband has brothers, she is married to them also A man in a polyandrous marriage can choose to leave it and take his own wife if his resources allow, but a wife in a polygynous marriage rarely can.

Polyandry exists in conditions of extreme poverty or female shortage. Among the polyandrous Todas of India there are often two males for every female, mainly because of the polygyny practiced by the boudoir bandits of the upper classes. Unlike monogamy in the United States, polyandry is not a valued marriage form in cultures where it is practiced; rather it is a practice born out of economic necessity (Tibet is the largest polyandrous culture). As economic conditions improve in such cultures there is a decline in polyandry. When sheer survival becomes less of a concern, humans come to conform more to the mating norms of other mammals and become either monogamous or polygynous. Having no natural biological basis, polyandry is an anthropological curiosity destined for extinction.

As evidenced by its wide incidence and its popularity as a perquisite of the privileged, polygyny probably does have a natural basis. If it were not it wouldn't need laws to prevent it. Laws exist either to get us to do things we naturally don't want to, or not to do things we are inclined to do. Polygyny simply doesn't fit the requirements of modern industrial societies. Even in Islam, the faith most supportive of polygyny, it is less and less encouraged. Fewer than 10 percent of Muslim marriages are polygnyous, and the trend is toward fewer and fewer as Islamic countries develop industrially. Monogamous marriage is a compromise between the male's natural inclinations and the requirements of modern society. That's good news for modern women, and probably for modern men also because each wife means another mother-in-law.

SO MANY WOMEN . . . SO LITTLE TIME:
THE SEX RATIO QUESTION

Speaking of sex, compromise, and social conditions, what kind of mating environment would you expect to develop when there is a significant excess of either men or women of marriageable age in a society such as ours that practices monogamy? Like anything else governed by the laws of supply and demand, scarcity determines value and abundance implies devaluation. When there is a significantly greater number of one sex than of the other, the sex with fewer members becomes a scarce resource and holds the power in dating and mating relationships. Now, if there were no differences in the mating strategies of men and women, scarcity would mean that although the members of the more numerous sex would have to try harder to land a mate, the essential moral nature of the mating environment would not change.

But mating strategies of men and women are very different, so in times when sex ratios are out of kilter mating environments are considerably altered. The effects of changing sex ratios on the customs and mores of society are so law-like that sociologists can predict marriage, divorce and illegitimacy rates from them, health professionals can predict venereal disease rates, and economists can predict the health of the travel, flower, greeting card, and restaurant markets.

Marcia Guttentag and Paul Secord, two psychologists, wrote a classic book dealing with this topic called *Too Many Women: The Sex Ratio Question*. This book surveyed the historical and sociological literature on cultures ranging from ancient Greece to modern America. They found in all cases that when males or females are freer to choose their behavior (because the sex ratio favors them) they will behave in ways compatible with their innate inclinations. When the sex ratio does not favor them, males and females must compromise their natural mating strategies and conform more to the strategy of the sex favored by the sex ratio or risk being mateless.

Because of immigration and "frontier blazing," every United States census until 1970 showed a significant excess of males; as high as nine men for every women in some western states in the nineteenth century. Such a sex ratio is obviously female favoring, and it helped to shape American values as they relate to marriage and the family. Under such a sex ratio men had to offer what women wanted, because if they didn't there were many others who would. Women were prized and respected, courtship was romantic, marriage was an attractive and permanent prospect, sexual intimacy was an expression of love, and adultery was morally unacceptable and legally punishable.

Guttentag and Secord showed that in the 1960 census there were still 111 men of marriageable age for every 100 women, but by 1970 the sex ratio had become male-favoring, with only 78 white men of marriageable age for every 100 white women. Things were even worse in the black community, with a sex ratio of 73 men for every 100 women. We all know what happened in the late nineteen-sixties and early nineteen-seventies—Sexual Revolution! Men had the upper hand, and they used it with a vengeance. A licentious environment ensued in which men, now following their natural inclinations, flitted from bed to bed and resisted romantic involvement as long as possible. Women had to compromise their inclinations and conform to the male strategy or risk being left out in the cold.

This is supported by the 1991 national survey of the number of sexual partners reported in *Family Planning Perspectives* mentioned in the last chapter. Subjects who were in their seventies in 1991 were at their sexual prime during the romantic, female-favoring decades of the forties and fifties. These folks (men and women combined) had a lifetime average of 3.51 sexual partners. The people with the highest average number of partners (9.71) were those in their sexual prime during the period of the largest female excess ever experienced in this country—the male-favoring, permissive years of the late nineteen-sixties. And most of these people have a few more years to go yet.

With skewed sex ratios, men and women may marry someone they may not otherwise consider. When the sex ratios of the late nineteenth and early twentieth centuries favored women, 70 percent of black-white marriages involved a white man and a black woman. With the excess of women in the nineteen-eighties, the racial composition of these marriages reversed, with 75 percent involving a white woman and a black man (interracial marriages are and have been, however, consistently rare, at less than 1 percent of all marriages). This left black women with even fewer marriage prospects, so they have had to compromise even more than white women. The illegitimate birth rate is a powerful indicator of this, with 66 percent of black births currently being illegitimate.

This doesn't mean that black women are naturally more promiscuous than white women. Data from slave plantations (where there were typically many more men than women) indicate that female slaves were quite "prudish," and that illegitimate births were rare. State-by-state comparisons show that black promiscuity is strongly a function of the ratio of males to females within them. In New York state, where there were 86 black males for every 100 black females in 1980, about 50 percent of black families were headed by a single female. In the same year in North Dakota, where there were 160 black males for every 100 black females, only 2.9 percent of black families were headed by a women—less than one-fifth the national white average of 17 percent. All this provides a powerful argument for differences in male/female sexual strategies and for the proposition that when men and women are free from the necessity of compromising with the opposite sex they will follow strategies that are consistent with their biological natures.

All historical and anthropological data relevant to this question show that permissive sexuality subverts the joys of romance, and the tenderness and caring that comes with it, just as surely as indiscriminately stuffing our face makes us fat, unappealing, and unappreciative of the place of food in our lives. When the female sexual strategy holds sway the world is a "kinder and gentler place." When the male strategy dominates, we get nasty creepies like AIDS and herpes, rap songs that demean and devalue women, and a general tearing of the fabric of the basic social institutions of marriage and the family. Let's hope the sex ratio becomes unskewed before we all come unscrewed.

SEX SELECTION AND THE GAMBLER'S FALLACY

Although we don't know why, given what we have just said about the effects of skewed sex ratios, about 75 percent of all couples contemplating their first child report that they would like it to be a boy. And couples are more likely to keep having children (trying for a boy) if they have had girls. In part this is due to a flawed concept called the gambler's fallacy. This fallacy holds that your luck just *has* to change the more you do things such as try to draw an ace, toss a head, or try for a boy baby. The trouble with this thinking is that we forget that each try constitutes events that are independent of one another. Say you want a boy and your previous three tries have produced girls. Since the probability of getting three girls in a row is quite small (it is actually about one in eight), you say to yourself that the probability of conceiving a boy on the next try must be quite high. This is totally wrong. Each birth, like each toss of a fair coin, is a completely random independent event. By this we mean that the outcome of previous conceptions in no way influences the outcome of subsequent conceptions. The odds of conceiving a girl (or boy) are still about fifty-fifty, regardless of how many other times a girl has been conceived, just as the odds of a head or tail is fifty-fifty on each toss of a fair coin regardless of previous outcomes.

But there's no need to fill your house with kids trying to get just one of the desired sex; there are ways of beating the odds. Fertility specialists have devised methods of sex selection that they claim are up to 80 percent successful. A good part of their method relies on the different attributes of the Y and X chomosome-bearing sperm. We have seen that the Y sperm is fast but vulnerable, and that the X sperm is slow but also hardier.

Since sperm has to meet egg to conceive, these specialists asked themselves, "How can we increase the odds that more Y or X sperm will get there first?" They noted that Orthodox Jews have a much higher than expected proportion of baby boys (130 boys to 100 girls, compared to the general Israeli ratio of 105 to 100). They also noted that for religious reasons Orthodox Jews don't engage in sexual intercourse until seven days after menstruation, putting the first post-menstrual intercourse at about the twelfth day of the wife's cycle—just before ovulation (shedding of the egg). This increases the chances of conceiving a boy in three ways. First, the period of abstinence raises the male's sperm count considerably. Second, at this time of the cycle the vaginal environment is slightly more alkaline, a condition shown experimentally to favor the Y sperm. Third, because the woman has just ovulated, the faster male sperm are more likely to penetrate the newly shed egg first.

This assumes that there are no sperm present from a previous intercourse swimming around waiting for ovulation. If there are, they are most likely to be the slower but less perishable X sperm. So if you want to maximize the probability of conceiving a boy you should abstain from intercourse for three to four days before ovulation. This allows time for old sperm to die; the competition then takes place only among the new batch of sperm.

One further boy-favoring technique learned from Orthodox Jews, whose writings advise them to "please" their women before themselves, is for the woman to achieve orgasm before the man. Orgasm opens the mouth of the uterus and encourages Y sperm to more quickly get out of the acid environment of the vagina, which is more damaging to them than to the X sperm, and to get into the more alkaline environment that they prefer.

To maximize the probability of a girl you should do the opposite. That is, you should have intercourse two or three days before ovulation and not again until two or three days after. This will lessen the overall probability of conception, but it will increase the probability of a girl if conception does take place. The female should also avoid orgasm (sorry) because, in addition to opening the mouth of the uterus, orgasm increases the flow of Y-favoring alkaline secretions in the vagina. See your gynecologist for more detailed instructions. In the mean time: happy loving, and good luck!

DIRTY PICTURES, DIRTY MINDS

Almost all mothers warn their daughters that "men only want one thing," and they're usually right. Women are understandably miffed at what they see as the male "objectification" of the female form, and this irritation is echoed in the lament, "You only want me for my body." The female "objects" men want are esthetically pleasing and utilitarian, or, put less pompously, they look good and can be used to satisfy sexual urges. We have seen that males possess brains for processing visual information to a greater degree than women, so it shouldn't be too surprising that they're more interested in gawking at the female form than females are in gazing at the male form. And, let's face it, ladies, you are co-conspirators in this because you do everything you can to make the sight more pleasing to them.

Women have brains better designed to process emotional information, so they're more interested in feeling (with the heart, not the hands) than in looking. This difference is readily seen in the preferred reading material of the sexes. Pornographic books (the books boys read with one hand) are almost exclusively bought and used by men. According to the *U.S. Commission on Obscenity and Pornography,* the porno business generates up to $700 million annually, and exists entirely for men. Romantic novels, on the other hand, are almost exclusively read by women. Even lesbians are not very interested in viewing crude sexual pictures of women.

Pornography, which typically involves a mixed bevy of bored nitwits poking each other in every conceivable orifice, is the ultimate example of impersonal, empty sex. You have to snicker, though, as these celluloid studs pull at their peckers in desperate attempts to defy gravity, and as their partners in slime fake orgasms as though they expect to win Oscar nominations. Although the evidence is sparse, some studies have linked heavy viewing of pornography to an increased likelihood of rape, an increased likelihood of abandoning stable monogamous relationships, and less love and appreciation of one's stable partner as men seek to emulate the excitement they come to associate with promiscuity. Regardless of the slimness of the evidence, we question whether regular viewers of the contortions of misaligned anatomy depicted in pornography can ever view women as other than a mere collection of interchangeable body parts.

Nude "beefcake" magazines fail to excite females the way "cheesecake" magazines excite males. With the advent of women's liberation, the female-oriented *Viva* magazine tried featuring male nudes, but the editors soon found these pinups to be letdowns when a survey of their readership found the nudes described as "ridiculous" or "distasteful." *Playgirl* magazine continues to publish naked beefcake, but the magazine has a large homosexual readership ("lookership"?) and many women read it for political reasons ("If men can have them, so can we!").

Being turned on to visual stimuli is easily assessed by measuring pupil dilation, an unambiguous physical indication of interest. When psychologists show men pictures of nude women, their pupils really "bug out"; when women are shown pictures of nude men, there is relatively little change, and the change is as likely to be constriction (indicating a physiological lack of interest) as dilation. Just the opposite is found when men and women are shown pictures of babies.

Males are "objectifiers" from the very earliest moments of life, and they respond to visually exciting stimulation to a greater degree than females. Male infants will respond with appreciative coos equally to human faces and mechanical objects, female infants generally respond with pleasure only to human faces. Asked to draw pictures, male children tend to draw objects such as cars and trucks more than people; girls are much more likely to draw people.

Go into your neighborhood public toilet and check out the graffiti. If you're a male, you are likely to find vulgar references to masturbation, homosexuality, and a variety of sexual practices, many of them illustrated to the best of their author's ability. As an occasional reader of this genre, I (Anthony) have yet to see tender expressions of love appearing on my cubicle walls. On the other hand, there is much tenderness expressed on cubicle walls that I (Grace) see, and what pictorial nastiness there is I suspect was put there by some male pervert. According to Dick, your cartoonist, girls' toilets in high school are an exception to this, but as with swearing, the female practice of drawing dirty graffiti diminishes after the madness of puberty. According to Grace, this is another way of saying that girls mature and boys don't.

PARAPHILIA: NAUGHTY VARIATIONS
ON THE SEXUAL THEME

The sexual impulses of individuals are sometimes directed into abnormal channels, some of them of such unsavory character that they are cataloged as diseases, or paraphilias. Paraphilias are disorders in which sexual feelings are aroused by unusual objects or situations that most people find unarousing, or even disgusting. The major paraphilias listed by the *Diagnostic and Statistical Manual of Mental Disorders* are pedophilia (sexual love of children), voyeurism (peeping Toms), exhibitionism (strutting your stuff), masochism ("Please beat me") and sadism ("Glad to oblige"). Other, rarer paraphilias that come under the general heading of fetishism include zoophilia (animals), necrophilia (corpses), coprophilia (feces), klismaphilia (enemas), and urophilia (urine). Although the DSM III lists sex ratios for all other mental disorders, as far as the paraphilias are concerned it says only: "Except for sexual masochism, in which the sex ratio is estimated twenty males for each female, the other paraphilias are practically never diagnosed for females, but some cases have been reported."

First let's take pedophilia, a clinical term often applied to child molesters. One team of psychologists reported that women were perpetrators of child molestation in only 9 out of 600 cases (1.5 percent) recently reported in New Hampshire and Vermont. In a survey of 48,700 sex offenses committed in the United Kingdom between 1975 and 1984, excluding prostitution and indecent exposure, only 1 percent were committed by women. Although women are not entirely immune from committing these offenses, case histories of such women almost always show them to be the result of severe character disorders, limited intelligence, and/or being forced to participate by a man. Female child molesters are quite different from typical women, but male child molesters are often indistinguishable from the typical man socially, psychologically, or intellectually. About 80 percent of the victims of child molesters are females.

Voyeurism and exhibitionism are difficult to untangle in terms of male/ female differences. Although the DSM III says that almost all such people are males, it could well be that some female strippers get a sexual jolt from exposing themselves, but we don't think of them as exhibitionists in the psychiatric sense. This possible double standard is also found in the legal world. Take the following two scenarios: (1) A women is walking by a darkened apartment; a light suddenly comes on in the apartment and the woman sees a man standing there buck naked. (2) A man is walking by a darkened apartment; a light suddenly comes on in the apartment and the man sees a women standing there in her birthday suit. If by chance an overly zealous police officer witnesses either scenario, guess which party will be cited. In scenario 1, the man will be cited for exhibitionism, and in scenario 2 he will be cited for being a peeping Tom. We take it for granted that in all such cases the man is the offender and the woman the offended, but we could be wrong on some occasions. Nevertheless, it remains true that women don't go around in dirty trenchcoats flashing their privy parts at unwitting males, nor do they sneak around in the dark trying to catch a peak at some unsuspecting guy's hairy backside.

Sadism and masochism are often lumped together as sadomasochism

because usually they need to be practiced together. A sadist can practice his cruelty on unwilling partners, however, and they are almost always women. A masochist, though, needs someone willing to inflict pain on him. This can be a man or a women, but most masochists feel more fully humiliated if the beatings and degradations are performed by women. Capitalizing on this are Amazon-type prostitutes who specialize in providing kinky men with a spanking good time. This specialty has obvious appeal for manhaters with an aggressive streak, but we'd hesitate to call them sadists in the sense that they derive sexual pleasure from their activities. They see it as making money, not whoopee.

Some folks who are neither sadists or masochists have occasional sexual fantasies about either inflicting or receiving pain. Kinsey reported that 20 percent of the men and 12 percent of the women reported fantasies of being dominated, and that 5 percent of the men and 2 percent of the women had at one time or another gotten pleasure out of inflicting sexual pain.

We think it fair to say that no other area of human activity more thoroughly separates men and women than the area of sexual perversion. When women engage in deviant sexual practices it is overwhelmingly for financial gain (prostitution, porno stardom), to please a loved partner, or because they have been forced into it. Rarely do women engage in it for their own sexual pleasure.

SEX AND CRIME

As far as criminality is concerned, women are, by a very large margin, the morally superior sex. In 1990, males accounted for 89 percent of all arrests for violent crimes and 76 percent of all arrests for property crimes. These crimes are broken down in Figure 9 by the eight major crimes that the FBI calls "index" crimes in its *Uniform Crime Report*. Among all other non-index crimes, prostitution is the only crime in which females predominate (70 percent), and don't forget that males are the customers for both male and female prostitutes.

Figure 9. 1990 Index Crime Figures for Males and Females

Violent Crime	Male	Female	Property Crime	Male	Female
Homicide	88%	12%	Burglary	93%	7%
Rape	99%	1%	Larceny/Theft	69%	31%
Robbery	92%	8%	Auto Theft	91%	9%
Aggravated Assault	86%	14%	Arson	87%	13%

Of the 20,040 criminal homicides committed in the United States in 1990, males were victims in 78 percent of the cases and females in 22 percent. Of the male victims, 85 percent were killed by other males and 15 percent were killed by females. Of the 4,399 female victims, 90 percent were killed by males, 9 percent by females, and 1 percent by "unknowns." Of the 3,960 females killed by men, 30 percent were killed by husbands or boyfriends. Four percent of all male victims were slain by wives or girlfriends. Romantic triangles account for the majority of males killing their wives or girlfriends. Most female killings of husbands and boyfriends (78 percent) occur in self-defense situations.

By law and convention, men historically had the right to physically chastise their wives as long as they didn't use a stick any thicker than their thumbs (the "rule of thumb") Even now that they no longer have that "right," sociologists estimate that one out of every six husbands beats his wife at least once a year and that one out of four will do so at least once during the marriage. The batteries of these grown-up Georgie Porgies is the single major cause of serious female injury. Rates of female abuse are even higher among unmarried couples living together. Believe it or not, there are also women who batter their husbands, although no reliable figures on the frequency of this phenomenon are available.

The number of women in American prisons rose 22 percent during the nineteen-eighties, but there are still about eighteen men behind bars for every one woman; fifty years ago the ratio was twenty-five to one. The explosive rise in drug use and trafficking accounts for most of the rise in female incarceration.

Unlike in male prisons, where rape and brutality are the norm, coerced sex in female prisons is rare. Homosexuality in male prisons is strongly sexually oriented and promiscuous, while lesbian liaisons in women's prisons emphasize attachment and caring, and minimize sexuality.

Studies show that women in prison who are inclined to lesbianism tend to get "married" and form "families," and sexual activity among women who were straight on the outside seldom goes beyond kissing and holding hands.

COME UP AND SEE ME SOMETIME

Another indication of the greater loyalty and nurturance of women is that wives and girlfriends are far more likely to visit their menfolk in prison than are husbands and boyfriends to visit their womenfolk. New York City's correctional commissioner said that husbands and boyfriends drop female convicts like "hot potatoes," but on the whole wives and girlfriends "stand by their man." In a study of seven federal prisons it was found that 50 percent of the women never had outside visitors, and that what visitors they had were overwhelmingly women. Only 25 percent of the male inmates never had visitors. Visiting days at prisons, whether the inmate is a man or a woman, are virtually all-female affairs.

One study found that although only 20 percent of female prison inmates are married, fully 80 percent of them are mothers. By way of contrast, 28 percent of male prisoners are married, and 60 percent of them are fathers.

Because female criminality is comparatively rare, it follows that female criminals are more atypical of their sex than male criminals are of theirs. Females are much more conforming in all their behavior than males, and to breach the threshold dividing deviance from nondeviance requires greater frequency and intensity of the various conditions said to be crime-causing for them. Although females are much less sensitive to crime-related factors outside the family, such as poverty and peer-group influences, they are sensitive to causes within the family. Even here, study after study shows that women bear the disabilities of a dysfunctional family better than men. One study of male and female sociopaths (more than 90 percent of all sociopaths are men) found that there existed "many more kinds of more frequent disruptive home experience in female sociopaths compared to male sociopaths." Another study comparing male and female juvenile delinquents found that the girls were 4.3 times more likely to be from broken homes and 3.2 times more likely to have been born out of wedlock, and were from families that were significantly lower on the socioeconomic scale. The natural aggressiveness, impulsiveness, thrill-seeking, and risk-taking of the male puts him at a much greater risk than the female for becoming a criminal.

ARE YOU MAN, WOMAN, OR IN-BETWEEN?

We have seen that masculinity and femininity are not either/or conditions, but rather lie on a continuous line ranging from extreme femininity to extreme masculinity. Neither of these extremes ("all woman" or "all man") is very appealing; it's good to have at least a portion of the attributes more common in the other sex. We don't mean that the Marines should be issued lipstick and lace or that the cheerleaders for the Dallas Cowboys should wear rayon longjohns over their unshaven legs. We just mean that we'd all be a little better off if we acknowledged those attributes we have but try to hide because we consider them either "unmasculine" or "unfeminine." We're all partly man and partly woman, and what little understanding there is between the sexes relies on that fact. Many psychologists insist that "androgynous" people (normal males and females who have more or less equal measures of "masculine" and "feminine" traits) are physically and mentally healthier and have higher self-esteem than rigidly sex-typed masculine males and feminine females. They stress that for the good of society, as well as the individual, it is particularly important for males to develop some of the nurturing, empathetic, and altruistic traits more typical of women.

Honestly scoring the questionnaire given below will give you a rough idea of how "masculine," "feminine," or "androgynous" you are.

Instructions: Indicate how each of the following statements describes you *most* of the time, by either strongly agreeing (SA), agreeing (A), being undecided (U), disagreeing (D), or strongly disagreeing (SD).

	SA	A	U	D	SD
1. I always defend my beliefs	□	□	□	□	□
2. I am quite affectionate	□	□	□	□	□
3. I consider myself pretty athletic	□	□	□	□	□
4. I often yield in matters of conflict	□	□	□	□	□
5. I am quite assertive	□	□	□	□	□
6. I am cheerful most of the time	□	□	□	□	□
7. I am an independent sort of person	□	□	□	□	□
8. I am quite shy	□	□	□	□	□
9. I am very self-reliant	□	□	□	□	□
10. I always like to look nice and presentable	□	□	□	□	□
11. I have a strong personality	□	□	□	□	□
12. I am very loyal to my friends of both sexes	□	□	□	□	□
13. I am quite forceful in my behavior	□	□	□	□	□
14. I consider myself quite feminine	□	□	□	□	□
15. I am analytical in my approach to problems	□	□	□	□	□
16. I am sympathetic to the problems of others	□	□	□	□	□
17. I consider myself a leader	□	□	□	□	□
18. I am quite sensitive to the needs of others	□	□	□	□	□
19. I am always willing to take risks	□	□	□	□	□

		SA	A	U	D	SD
20.	I am a very understanding person	☐	☐	☐	☐	☐
21.	I make decisions quickly and easily	☐	☐	☐	☐	☐
22.	I am a very compassionate person	☐	☐	☐	☐	☐
23.	I think I'm a pretty self-sufficient person	☐	☐	☐	☐	☐
24.	I am eager to soothe people's feelings	☐	☐	☐	☐	☐
25.	I have a dominating personality	☐	☐	☐	☐	☐
26.	I am quite soft-spoken	☐	☐	☐	☐	☐
27.	I consider myself quite masculine	☐	☐	☐	☐	☐
28.	I am a warm sort of person	☐	☐	☐	☐	☐
29.	I enjoy pornography	☐	☐	☐	☐	☐
30.	I am a tender sort of person	☐	☐	☐	☐	☐
31.	I am quite aggressive	☐	☐	☐	☐	☐
32.	I don't believe in "one-night stands"	☐	☐	☐	☐	☐
33.	I am a pretty individualistic sort of person	☐	☐	☐	☐	☐
34.	I rarely use bad language	☐	☐	☐	☐	☐
35.	I am a pretty competitive sort of person	☐	☐	☐	☐	☐
36.	I really love children	☐	☐	☐	☐	☐
37.	I am very ambitious	☐	☐	☐	☐	☐
38.	I am a gentle sort of person	☐	☐	☐	☐	☐
39.	I can point to east or west wherever I am	☐	☐	☐	☐	☐
40.	I find English easier than math	☐	☐	☐	☐	☐

Scoring: Give yourself 4 points for every SA answer, 3 for every A, 2 for every U, 1 for every D, and O for every SD. The sum of the odd-numbered items is your masculinity score, the sum of even-numbered items is your femininity score. Add 1 point to your femininity score for every item you have marked "undecided." Decide whether you are low, medium, or high on both scores as follows:

Masculinity	**Femininity**
0–27 = low	0–27 = low
28–54 = medium	28–54 = medium
55–80 = high	55–80 = high

Subtract your femininity score from your masculinity score. Determine whether you are "masculine," "feminine," or "androgynous" by comparing your score with those given below.

–80 through –27 = feminine

–26 through +26 = androgynous

+27 through +80 = masculine

Bibliography

As we indicated in the preface, we drew from far too many sources to list them all here. Listed here are the major works that we found most useful.

American Psychiatric Association. *Diagnostic and Statistical Manual of Mental Disorders III.* Washington, D.C.: APA, 1987.

Bardwick, Judith. *The Psychology of Women.* New York: Harper & Row, 1971.

Bell, Alan, Martin Weinberg, and Sue Kiefer Hammersmith. *Sexual Preference: Its Development in Men and Women.* Alfred C. Kinsey Institute for Sex Research, Bloomington, Ind.: Indiana University Press, 1981.

Diagram Group. *Man's Body: An Owner's Manual.* New York: Bantam, 1976.

———. *The Brain: A User's Manual.* New York: Bantam, 1983.

Durden-Smith, Jo, and Diane deSimone. *Sex and the Brain.* New York: Arbor House, 1983.

Edlin, Gordon. *Human Genetics: A Modern Synthesis.* Boston: Jones and Bartlett, 1990.

Federal Bureau of Investigation. *Uniform Crime Reports.* Washington, D.C.: U.S. Department of Justice, 1991.

Gebhard, Paul, and A. Johnson. *The Kinsey Data: Marginal Tabulations of the 1938–1963 Interviews Conducted by the Institute for Sex Research.* Philadelphia: Saunders, 1979.

Guttentag, Marcia, and Paul Secord. *Too Many Women: The Sex Ratio Question.* Beverly Hills, Calif.: Sage, 1983.

Hite, Shere. *The Hite Report: A Nationwide Study of Female Sexuality.* New York: Macmillan, 1980.

Hite, Shere. *The Hite Report on Male Sexuality*. New York: Ballantine, 1981.

Hoyenga, Katherine, and Kermit Hoyenga. *The Question of Sex Differences*. Boston: Little, Brown, 1979.

Hutt, Corinne. *Males and Females*. Middlesex, England: Penguin, 1975.

Kachigan, Sam. *The Sexual Matrix: Boy Meets Girl on the Evolutionary Scale*. New York: Radius.

Khan, Aman, and Joseph Cataio. *Men and Women in Biological Perspective: A Review of the Literature*. New York: Praeger, 1984.

Kolb, Bryan, and Ian Wishaw. *Fundamentals of Human Neurophysiology*. New York: W. H. Freeman, 1985.

Kramer, Laura. *The Sociology of Gender*. New York: St. Martin's, 1991.

Lang, Theo. *The Difference between a Man and a Woman*. New York: John Day, 1971.

Mellen, Sydney. *The Evolution of Love*. San Francisco: W. H. Freeman, 1981.

Moir, Ann, and David Jessel. *Brain Sex: The Real Difference between Men and Women*. New York: Lyle Stuart, 1991.

Montagu, Ashley. *The Natural Superiority of Women*. New York: Collier, 1974.

Nicholson, John. *Men & Women: How Different Are They?* Oxford, England: Oxford University Press, 1984.

Saxton, Lloyd. *The Individual, Marriage, and the Family*. Belmont, Calif.: Wadsworth, 1986.

Symons, Donald. *The Evolution of Human Sexuality*. New York: Oxford University Press.

Tavris, Carol, and Carole Offir. *The Longest War: Sex Differences in Perspective*. New York: Harcourt Brace Jovanovich, 1977.

Tavris, Carol, and Susan Sadd. *The Redbook Report on Female Sexuality*. New York: Delacorte, 1977.

Teitelbaum, Michael. *Sex Differences: Social and Biological Perspectives*. Garden City, N.Y.: Anchor, 1976.

Thompson, Jack. *The Psychobiology of Emotions*. New York: Plenum, 1988.

Wagenvoord, James, and Peyton Bailey. *Women: A Book for Men*. New York: Avon, 1979.

Walsh, Anthony. *The Science of Love: Understanding Love and its Effects on Mind and Body*. Buffalo, N.Y.: Prometheus, 1991.

Wilson, Glenn. *Love and Instinct*. New York: Quill, 1983.